高职高专公共英语
智慧云版系列教材

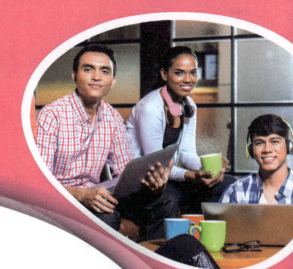

新发展高职英语
综合教程 ③

New Development

College English
Comprehensive Course

总主编 王永祥
主　编 张　剑　罗柳萍

副主编　秦熙治　吴　可
　　　　周　红　黄　珣
编　者　张　剑　罗柳萍　秦熙治
　　　　吴　可　周　红　黄　珣

北京理工大学出版社
BEIJING INSTITUTE OF TECHNOLOGY PRESS

版权专有　侵权必究

图书在版编目（CIP）数据

新发展高职英语综合教程. 3 / 张剑, 罗柳萍主编
. -- 北京:北京理工大学出版社，2021.11
高职高专公共英语智慧云版系列教材 / 王永祥主编
ISBN 978-7-5763-0746-7

Ⅰ.①新… Ⅱ.①张… ②罗… Ⅲ.①英语–高等职业教育–教材 Ⅳ.①H319.39

中国版本图书馆CIP数据核字 (2021) 第247912号

出版发行 / 北京理工大学出版社有限责任公司	
社　　址 / 北京市海淀区中关村南大街5号	
邮　　编 / 100081	
电　　话 /（010）68914775（总编室）	
（010）82562903（教材售后服务热线）	
（010）68944723（其他图书服务热线）	
网　　址 / http://www.bitpress.com.cn	
经　　销 / 全国各地新华书店	
印　　刷 / 沂南县汶凤印刷有限公司	
开　　本 / 889毫米 × 1194毫米　1/16	
印　　张 / 12.25	责任编辑 / 武丽娟
字　　数 / 302千字	文案编辑 / 武丽娟
版　　次 / 2021年11月第1版　2021年11月第1次印刷	责任校对 / 刘亚男
定　　价 / 49.80元	责任印制 / 施胜娟

图书出现印装质量问题，请拨打售后服务热线，本社负责调换

FOREWORD

　　系统功能语言学创始人韩礼德（M. A. K. Halliday）在其"以语言为基础的学习理论"（Towards a Language-based Theory of Learning, 1993）一文中指出，语言学习包含三个方面：学习语言（learning language）、通过语言学习（learning through language）、学习语言知识（learning about language）。学习语言知识很容易做到，绝大多数外语教材和外语课堂均能实现。而广大外语教育工作者并不满足于此，他们懂得，外语学习的目的不仅仅是获得各种语言知识，还需要掌握各种语言技能，需要能够真正听懂外语、讲好外语、读懂外语、写好外语，即真正地"学习语言"，从而培养交际能力。除了"学习语言"和"学习语言知识"以外，语言学习还有一个非常重要的目的，那就是"通过语言学习"。对学习者而言，所谓"通过语言学习"就是运用语言学习各种不同领域的专业知识和技能。因此，高职英语教学必然包含一项重要任务——帮助学生运用英语学习各种职场知识。

　　为全面贯彻《高等职业教育专科英语课程标准》（2021版）和《高职高专教育英语课程教学基本要求》的精神，并基于上文所述理念，编者编写了《新发展高职英语综合教程》系列教材。本套教材涵盖高等职业教育专科阶段英语学科必须具备的四大核心素养：职场涉外沟通、多元文化交流、语言思维提升和自主学习完善。通过本套教材的学习，学生能够达到课程标准所设定的四项学科核心素养的发展目标，即职场涉外沟通目标、多元文化交流目标、语言思维提升目标和自主学习完善目标。

　　本套教材共3册。第1册将高职学生在校三年主要的典型环节缩影于第一学期，让学生在开学之初适应中职或者高中阶段与高职阶段学习的同时，对未来高职三年的整体学习获得宏观了解，并树立职业目标，做好职业规划。第2册则聚焦各行各业中的共核技能并进行提炼和整合，侧重具体的职业知识和职业技能，重点培养学生的专业知识和职业能力。第3册主要突出职业提升，在职业提升中兼顾素养提升和学业提升。

本套教材内容丰富，包括职业与个人、职业与社会、职业与环境三大主题。每册每个单元围绕具体主题进行不同模块的设计，包括热身练习（Warm-up）、主课文（Reading A）、听说（Listening and speaking）、副课文（Reading B）、应用写作（Applied writing）、项目操练（Project performing）、语法（Grammar）、自我评价（Self-evaluation）、文化（Culture）等。这些模块既有语言知识（语法）和语言技能（听说读写）的训练，也有语言在职场中的具体运用。

《新发展高职英语综合教程》践行以运用为导向的高职英语教学理念，助力广大高职院校英语教师实现高职英语教学中语言知识、语言能力与语言运用的融合，实现对韩礼德所阐述的语言学习三个方面（"学习语言""通过语言学习"和"学习语言知识"）的全覆盖。

王永祥

2021年夏于南京仙林湖畔

PREFACE

　　《新发展高职英语综合教程》是由北京理工大学出版社设计研发、由国内英语教育专家和多所高校骨干教师共同参与设计和编写的具有时代特色和国际水准的高职高专英语教材。

　　《新发展高职英语综合教程 3》是这套教材中的最后一册，难度较前两册有一定的提升，可以作为高职高专学校的英语必修课教材或英语拓展教材。本教材在第一、二册的基础上，突出职业能力的提升、思维能力的提升、倡导终身学习、培养国匠之才，话题包括：中华美食与文化、职场礼仪文化、非遗传承与区域发展、国潮崛起、职业安全与职业道德、终生学习。希望通过本教材的学习，进一步提升学生的职场涉外沟通能力和职业素养，同时培养学生的社会责任感和家国情怀。

　　本教材针对高职高专院校学生的特点，教材设计方面内容丰富多彩，趣味性和知识性相结合，文字材料和多媒体材料相结合，线上与线下学习相结合，课堂学习与自主学习相结合，不但能够满足各类高校不同层次学生的需求，还能满足不同教学模式的需求。本教材共有六个单元，每个单元围绕同一主题展开，由热身练习（Warm-up）、主课文（Reading A）、听说（Listening and speaking）、副课文（Reading B）、单元练习（Comprehensive exercises）、应用写作（Applied writing）、项目操练（Project performing）、语法（Grammar）、自我评价（Self-evaluation）、文化（Culture）十个板块组成，主题特色鲜明，涉及职业与个人、职业与社会以及职业与世界各方面的关系。

　　本教材的练习循序渐进，形式多样，可供教师选择用于课堂教学和课外作业。练习充分考虑到学生的实际需求，提供了充足的辅助手段。除了聚焦课文中的词汇、语法以及篇章理解外，还特别鼓励学生基于课文，结合个人、职场以及社会现象进行讨论，发表自己的观点，提升辩证思维能力。教师可以组织以学生为中心的各种课堂任务和项目实践活动，以多种形式实现本教材的教学目标。

《新发展高职英语综合教程3》突破了传统高职高专英语教学模式的局限性，在课程思政、思辨能力培养以及职业素养提升方面作出了有益的尝试。

本教材是集体智慧的结晶。王永祥教授担任总主编，负责教材的总框架设计、选文审核及定稿审核等工作。张剑、罗柳萍组织了本书的编写，并对全书统编定稿。本书的编写分工如下：黄珣编写第一单元；周红编写第二单元；罗柳萍编写第三单元；秦熙治编写第四单元；吴可编写第五单元；张剑编写第六单元。

本教材的素材大多选自国内外媒体的网上资源，并对文章进行了改编，特向作者表示诚挚的感谢。北京理工大学出版社各位编辑和同仁对本书的出版给予了大力支持和帮助，在此一并表示感谢。

由于时间仓促，本教材在编写过程中难免存在错误和不当之处，敬请广大读者和同行批评指正！

编　者

2021年9月

Unit 1
Chinese Cuisine and Food Culture

Warm-up	2
Reading A	4
Listening and speaking	8
Reading B	12
Applied writing	20
Project performing	22
Grammar	23
Self-evaluation	28
Culture	29

Unit 2
Workplace Etiquettes

Warm-up	32
Reading A	35
Listening and speaking	39
Reading B	42
Applied writing	49
Project performing	51
Grammar	52
Self-evaluation	55
Culture	56

Unit 3
Intangible Cultural Heritage and Regional Development

Warm-up	60
Reading A	62
Listening and speaking	67
Reading B	72
Applied writing	79
Project performing	81
Grammar	83
Self-evaluation	85
Culture	86

Unit 4
The Rise of Guochao

Warm-up	88
Reading A	91
Listening and speaking	94
Reading B	98
Applied writing	104
Project performing	106
Grammar	108
Self-evaluation	110
Culture	111

Unit 5
Work Ethics and Job Security

Warm-up	114
Reading A	115
Listening and speaking	119
Reading B	122
Applied writing	129
Project performing	130
Grammar	132
Self-evaluation	135
Culture	136

CONTENTS 3

Unit 6 **Life-long Learning**	Warm-up	138
	Reading A	139
	Listening and speaking	143
	Reading B	146
	Applied writing	152
	Project performing	154
	Grammar	156
	Self-evaluation	158
	Culture	159

Word List	New words & expressions	162
	Glossary	173
	Phrases & expressions	183

Unit 1
Chinese Cuisine and Food Culture

Learning objectives

After studying this unit, you should be able to:
- get familiar with the words and expressions concerning Chinese food and Chinese cuisine;
- have an in-depth understanding of Chinese cuisine and food culture;
- write a résumé in English;
- master how to use the inverted sentences.

Warm-up

Task 1 Watch the video and discuss the following questions with your classmates.

1. What food have you heard of in the video?
2. What is your home town's special food? And what is your favorite food? Some key words and phrases are listed for you.

special food 特色美食	delicacy 佳肴	delicious 美味的	typical style 地道风味
crisp 酥脆的	tasty 可口的	tender 鲜嫩的	clear 清淡的
strong 浓烈的	spicy 香辣的		

Unit 1 | Chinese Cuisine and Food Culture

Task 2 The following pictures show some traditional Chinese dishes. Match each picture with its name in English.

( ) 1. steamed fish   ( ) 2. hot pot
( ) 3. fried rice   ( ) 4. roast duck
( ) 5. beef in oyster sauce   ( ) 6. roast suckling pig
( ) 7. blanched chicken   ( ) 8. twice-cooked pork slices
( ) 9. braised minced pork balls in brown sauce

Reading A

Pre-reading questions

1. What is staple food? What is non-staple food?
2. What impact does the use of ingredients have on Chinese food?

Ingredients used in Chinese food

Chinese people have categories of staple and non-staple food. In Southern China, where rice farming is common, the staple food is rice. Whereas, in Northern China, where wheat farming is more prevalent, staple food consists of flour-based sustenance such as noodles, dumplings, steamed buns (*mantou*) and pancakes. Other staple foods include grains, cereals, and sweet potatoes. Chinese food is not divided by first, second and third course, but rather by a cold dish (served first), followed by soup and then hot dish (usually main course). The Chinese people do not consider desserts as the final course but as snacks usually taken between meals. Fruit is usually served at the end of the meal.

In addition to staple food, meat, vegetables, and fruits are also an important part of the Chinese diet. The ingredients used in Chinese cooking are very important for authentic taste and overall feel of the food. Chinese cooking is a fusion of taste, aroma, aesthetics, and form that is achieved through using various utensils, cooking techniques, spices, sauces, and oils.

Chinese prefer cooking in a wok, a shallow bowl-shaped frying pan with thin walls. A steamer and rice cooker are also popular cooking utensils in China. They employ various cooking techniques such as stir-frying, steaming, boiling, braising, simmering, deep-frying, pickling, stewing and smoking. Important sauces include

both white and dark soy sauce, Shaoxing wine, oyster sauce, Chinkiang or rice vinegar and hoisin sauce. Peanut and sesame oils are also two of the essential Chinese cooking ingredients. Their food is also infused with ginger and garlic flavors, and spices such as salt, white pepper, dried chili peppers, and Sichuan peppercorns are an integral part of Chinese cuisine.

The Chinese people believe that food is not only vital for providing energy and nutritional benefits, but also for its medicinal purposes and properties. This is known as therapy by diet. It is believed that whatever we eat has an influence on the human body and some things are more effective in treating certain kinds of ailments and illnesses. For example, it is believed by the Chinese people that ginger is a very good source of treating and avoiding cold.

Similarly, many ingredients and herbs are used in the cooking by the Chinese local not only to make the food tasty but also for the body to absorb its medicinal properties to prevent and cure illness.

The Chinese believe medicine has a toxic effect on the body and should be avoided as much as possible. One may turn to medicine if treatment through diet therapy has failed.

(426 words)

New words

*category	/ˈkætəgəri/	n.	（人或事物的）类别，种类
*staple	/ˈsteɪpl/	a.	主要的；基本的；重要的
*prevalent	/ˈprevələnt/	a.	流行的；普遍存在的；盛行的
sustenance	/ˈsʌstənəns/	n.	食物；营养；养料
*ingredient	/ɪnˈɡriːdiənt/	n.	成分；（尤指烹饪）原料
▲authentic	/ɔːˈθentɪk/	a.	真正的；真实的；逼真的
▲fusion	/ˈfjuːʒn/	n.	融合；熔接；结合
*aroma	/əˈrəʊmə/	n.	芳香；香味
aesthetic	/iːˈsθetɪk/	n.	（审）美学；美的哲学
▲utensil	/juːˈtensl/	n.	（家庭）用具，器皿
wok	/wɒk/	n.	炒菜锅
*essential	/ɪˈsenʃl/	a.	必要的；必不可少的；根本的
		n.	必不可少的东西；必需品；要点

▲integral	/ˈɪntɪgrəl/	a.	必需的；不可或缺的
		n.	整体
*vital	/ˈvaɪtl/	a.	必不可少的；对……极重要的；充满生机的
*nutritional	/njuˈtrɪʃnl/	a.	（食物中）营养的，营养成分的
*property	/ˈprɒpəti/	n.	所有物；财产；不动产
▲therapy	/ˈθerəpi/	n.	治疗；疗法
*diet	/ˈdaɪət/	n.	日常饮食；规定饮食（为健康或减肥等目的）
		v.	节食；按规定饮食
*influence	/ˈɪnfluəns/	n.	影响；作用；有影响的人（或事物）
		v.	影响；对……起作用；支配；左右
ailment	/ˈeɪlmənt/	n.	轻病；小恙
*treat	/triːt/	v.	处理；治疗；把……看作
*avoid	/əˈvɔɪd/	v.	避免；防止；躲避
*herb	/hɜːb/	n.	药草；香草；草本植物
▲absorb	/əbˈzɔːb/	v.	吸收（液体、气体等）
*prevent	/prɪˈvent/	v.	阻止；阻碍；阻挠
*cure	/kjʊə(r)/	v.	治愈，治好（疾病）；解决（问题）
		n.	药物；疗法；治疗
toxic	/ˈtɒksɪk/	a.	有毒的；引起中毒的
		n.	毒物；毒剂

🗨 Phrases & expressions

consist of	由……组成
be divided by	按……划分
in addition to	加之；另外；又
be infused with	融入

🖉 Proper names

Chinkiang vinegar	镇江香醋（中国江苏省镇江市特产，中国国家地理标志产品）
hoisin sauce	海鲜酱（一种调味品，能够抑腥提鲜，是烹制海鲜或生鲜肉类的优质调味料）

生词数	生词率	*B级词汇	*A级词汇	▲四、六级词汇	超纲词汇
27	6.3%	10	6	6	5

Unit 1 | Chinese Cuisine and Food Culture 7

Notes

Cooking techniques

stir-frying（翻炒）　　　　quick-frying（快炒）　　　　sauting（快炒，嫩煎）
steaming（清蒸）　　　　 boiling（水煮）　　　　　　　braising（焖，烧）
simmering（小火慢煮）　　deep-frying（油炸）　　　　　pickling（腌制）
stewing（炖，煨）　　　　 smoking（烟熏）

After-reading tasks

Task 1 Tick off the following factors which are combined in a fusion of Chinese cooking according to Reading A.

☐ 1. taste　　☐ 2. aroma　　☐ 3. aesthetics　　☐ 4. utensils　　☐ 5. sauces
☐ 6. spices　 ☐ 7. oils　　　☐ 8. herbs　　　　 ☐ 9. medicine
☐ 10. cooking techniques

Task 2 Read Reading A again and decide whether the following statements are true or false.

(　) 1. The staple food in the north and south of China is different.
(　) 2. Chinese food is divided by a cold dish (served first), followed by soup and then hot dish (usually main course).
(　) 3. Dessert is usually served at the end of the meal.
(　) 4. Butter and ketchup are also two of the essential Chinese cooking ingredients.
(　) 5. Chinese people believe that food as therapy by diet can also treat illnesses.

Listening and speaking

Task 1 Listen to Dialogue 1 and number the food names in the order you have heard.

In the Chinese restaurant where buffet breakfast is served, Mr. Smith (S) approaches the long stand (长桌) with a plate in his hand. He asks the waiter(W) with great curiosity.

S: Do you serve buffet for Chinese breakfast?

W: Certainly, sir. It is all here on the long stand. This is fresh milk and that is ___1___.

S: Good. I'd like some Chinese tea.

W: Well, this tea pot is for black tea and that one for ___2___.

S: Oh, I see. Oolong tea is longevity tea, isn't it?

W: Yes, it is. And over here are several kinds of ___3___. This is ___4___ stuffed with red bean puree, and that is with diced shrimps, bamboo shoots and mushroom.

S: Great. I will have both. And what is that?

W: It's fried ___5___ stuffed with shredded cabbage and pork. It's best eaten with some ___6___.

S: Terrific.

W: Besides, we have two kinds of noodles. One is ___7___ with different dressing, and the other, ___8___ in Shanghai style.

S: I see. Is that cereal?

W: I'm afraid not, sir. That's Chinese ___9___. You may enjoy it with delicious Yangzhou pickles. Also available is ___10___.

S: Wonderful. I will taste something of everything here.

W: Bon appetit!

( ) **A.** noodle soup ( ) **B.** steamed dumpling

( ) **C.** plain porridge ( ) **D.** Oolong tea

( ) **E.** stir-fried noodles ( ) **F.** porridge with minced pork and preserved egg

( ) **G.** vinegar ( ) **H.** spring roll

( ) **I.** soybean milk ( ) **J.** dim sum

Unit 1 | Chinese Cuisine and Food Culture 9

Task 2 Listen to Dialogue 2 and fill in the blanks.

The waiter (W) is explaining something to Johnson (J).

W: Are you ready to order, sir?

J: Yes, I'd like to try some Chinese food.

W: We serve Chinese food here, but I'm not sure which style you prefer.

J: I ___1___ Chinese food.

W: Well, ___2___ of Chinese food is harmony in color, flavor, taste, shape, or even the use of utensils.

J: That sounds terrific.

W: To be more specific, Chinese food ___3___ eight big cuisines or say eight styles, such as Guangdong food, Shandong food, Sichuan food, etc.

J: Is there any difference between Guangdong food and Shandong food?

W: Yes, Guangdong food is lighter while Shandong food is heavy and spicy.

J: Is the world famous Beijing roast duck a speciality of Shandong cuisine?

W: Exactly.

J: How about Sichuan food?

W: Most Sichuan dishes are spicy and hot, and they ___4___.

J: Oh, really? I like hot food. So what's your ___5___ for me?

W: I think Mapo beancurd, shredded meat in chili sauce, and hot and sour soup are quite special.

J: Thank you for your information.

Task 3 Role-play in pairs according to the situation given below.

Diner: Ask if the restaurant serves Chinese food for buffet.
   Ask what soybean milk is and what dim sum means.
   Ask how many kinds of rice porridge.
   Ask what kind of egg the preserved egg is.
   Ask how many kinds of dumplings.

Waiter: Explain what dim sum means.
   There are two kinds of rice porridge.
   Explain soybean milk and preserved egg.
   Recommend two kinds of dumplings.

10 新发展高职英语综合教程 ❸

Task 4 Listen to Dialogue 3 and answer the following questions.

1. What party is Robert invited to?

   _____

2. Is this a formal party?

   _____

3. What is usually eaten at a Chinese birthday party?

   _____

4. Is there any special meaning for one to have noodles to celebrate one's birthday?

   _____

5. If you celebrate your birthday, what food would you choose, longevity noodles or birthday cake?

   _____

Task 5 Listen to Dialogue 4 and fill in the blanks.

Fang (F) is telling David (D) how a Chinese banquet is served.

D: Mr. Fang, I was told a Chinese banquet always ____1____ us big eaters. I've never experienced that. Tell me something about it.

F: It's a pleasure. A Chinese banquet usually starts with ____2____. It can be mixed seafood, poultry or vegetables. Then come to seafood soup.

D: That's all?

F: Not yet. Following the seafood soup, there will be a chicken dish, a prawn, a duck, or a pigeon dish. Then comes ____3____, always followed by a fish. When you see fish, you know that all the main dishes have been served and the dinner will ____4____ rice. Lastly, there are two or four kinds of dim sum for dessert, then fresh fruit and a cup of hot tea to conclude the banquet.

D: Oh, it's a feast to feed a small army. Well, why do you always have the fish as the last main dish?

F: In Chinese, the word "fish" is a pun to "____5____".

Task 6 Role-play in pairs according to the situation given below.

Guest: You come to discuss the menu for a banquet.
You check two set menus.
You prefer the cold dishes of Menu A.
You want to have main dishes on Menu B, but you make some changes.
You check the new menu and feel satisfied.

Waiter: You have got two set menus ready.
You make certain suggestions for main dishes.
You explain the difference in price.
You have the new menu typed.

Reading B

📖 Pre-reading questions

1. Can you name some traditional Chinese festivals that are celebrated for family reunion?
2. In your hometown, what food do you prepare or eat for the Spring Festival?

Best food on Chinese New Year

Chinese New Year or the Spring Festival marks the beginning of a new year on the Chinese traditional calendar. Chinese New Year is also celebrated worldwide in regions and countries with significant Overseas Chinese or Sinophone populations. These countries include Singapore, Indonesia, Malaysia, Myanmar, Thailand, Cambodia, the Philippines, and Mauritius, as well as many in North America and Europe.

Chinese New Year is associated with several myths and customs. The evening preceding Chinese New Year's Day is frequently regarded as an occasion for Chinese families to gather for the annual reunion dinner. It is also traditional for every family to thoroughly clean their house, in order to sweep away any ill-fortune and to make way for incoming good luck. Another custom is the decoration of windows and doors with red paper-cuts and couplets. Other activities include lighting firecrackers and giving money in red paper envelopes.

Food, of course, is a very important part of the New Year celebrations. Foods that are associated with good fortune, wealth, health and prosperity are often a part of the Chinese New Year celebrations. Below is a list of the best Chinese food items that are most commonly prepared during the spring festival.

1. SPRING ROLLS

Spring rolls are a part of the Spring Festival and can appear on the table as a dinner dish, appetizer or snack. More specifically, they are eaten on the first day of spring. The wrap of the spring rolls is of flour. The filling can be of personal choice but is typically of meat, Chinese cabbage, shiitake, carrots, and seasoning. Steamed, baked or fried, spring rolls are an important part of the New Year Dinner.

2. DUMPLINGS

Another well-known dish, dumplings are the northern equivalent of spring rolls. In addition to the joy of eating delicious food, the making process is a family bonding activity too. During New Year's preparations, every member of the family participates and wraps dumplings. It traditionally includes any type of meat, vegetables, eggs, and seasoning. Every special occasion usually has dumplings, but they are the most significant during Chinese New Year.

3. NOODLES

For Chinese New Year, people like to eat long noodles. The Mandarin word for noodles means "longevity noodles". The longer the noodle, the longer your life will be. With noodles, there is great flexibility for sides and ingredients. Many vegetables and meats have symbolic meanings as well. For example:

- Eggs: big and healthy family
- Lobster: endless money rolling in
- Shrimp: fortune and wealth
- Roasted pig: peace
- Duck: loyalty
- Tofu: happiness and fortune for the entire family
- Fish: surplus and wealth

4. STEAMED FISH

Fish is a must for the Chinese New Year. This is because the Mandarin word for the words "fish" and "surplus" have similar pronunciations. People will steam a whole fish for the New Year dinner. This is to prolong the surplus and make the future prosperous as well. A whole fish also represents a harmonious and whole family.

5. STEAMED CHICKEN

A whole chicken is another symbol of family. Rich in protein, one chicken is enough to feed an entire family. It represents reunion and rebirth. To express this auspicious meaning, people keep the head and claws. After cooking, people will first offer the chicken to their ancestors.

6. NIANGAO

Also known as "rice cake" or "New Year cake" in English, *Niangao* has the same pronunciation as the Chinese word for tall/high. It's a wish to be successful and "higher" each year, that every year will be better than the last.

7. HOT POT

Hot pot is another one of the best Chinese dishes. It's simply a bubbling pot and plates of uncooked meat and vegetables. You can choose whatever you like to throw into the pot. Wait until it's cooked, take it out and eat. Part of the flavor comes from the broth you choose in the pot. The other part is your dipping sauce. There are several hot pot sauces. Everything mentioned in this article can be included as an option to be put into the hot pot.

(674 words)

New words

*calendar	/ˈkælɪndə(r)/	n.	日历；挂历；日程表
*region	/ˈriːdʒən/	n.	地区，区域，地方；行政
*significant	/sɪɡˈnɪfɪkənt/	a.	有重大意义的；显著的
Sinophone	/ˈsaɪnəʊfəʊn/	n.	华语语系；译意风
*myth	/mɪθ/	n.	神话
*occasion	/əˈkeɪʒn/	n.	场合；特别的事情（或仪式、庆典）
*annual	/ˈænjuəl/	a.	每年的；一年一次的；年度的
*reunion	/ˌriːˈjuːniən/	n.	重逢；团聚；聚会；相聚；团圆
*decoration	/ˌdekəˈreɪʃn/	n.	装饰品；装饰图案；装饰风格
couplet	/ˈkʌplət/	n.	对句（相连的两行长度相等的诗句）；对联
*firecracker	/ˈfaɪəkrækə(r)/	n.	鞭炮；爆竹

*envelope	/ˈenvələʊp/	n.	信封；塑料封套；塑料封皮
*appear	/əˈpɪə(r)/	v.	显得；看来；似乎；出现；呈现；显现
*appetizer	/ˈæpɪtaɪzə(r)/	n.	（餐前的）开胃品，开胃饮料
*snack	/snæk/	n.	点心；小吃；快餐
*wrap	/ræp/	n.	包裹（或包装）材料
		v.	包；裹；用……包裹（或包扎、覆盖等）
shiitake	/ʃɪˈtɑːki/	n.	香菇；香蕈
*seasoning	/ˈsiːzənɪŋ/	n.	调味品；作料
▲equivalent	/ɪˈkwɪvələnt/	a.	（价值、数量、意义、重要性等）相等的，相同的
▲bonding	/ˈbɒndɪŋ/	n.	人与人之间的关系
		v.	使……结合；使……联结
*participate	/pɑːˈtɪsɪpeɪt/	v.	参加；参与
*Mandarin	/ˈmændərɪn/	n.	（中文）普通话
*longevity	/lɒnˈdʒevəti/	n.	长寿；长命；持久
*flexibility	/ˌfleksəˈbɪləti/	n.	柔韧性；灵活性；弹性
*symbolic	/sɪmˈbɒlɪk/	a.	作为象征的；象征性的
*loyalty	/ˈlɔɪəlti/	n.	忠诚；忠实；忠心耿耿
▲surplus	/ˈsɜːpləs/	n.	过剩；剩余；盈余
		a.	过剩的；剩余的；多余的
*prolong	/prəˈlɒŋ/	v.	延长
▲prosperous	/ˈprɒspərəs/	a.	繁荣的；成功的；兴旺的
*represent	/ˌreprɪˈzent/	v.	代表；作为……的代言人
*harmonious	/hɑːˈməʊniəs/	a.	友好和睦的；和谐的；协调的
*protein	/ˈprəʊtiːn/	n.	蛋白质
*entire	/ɪnˈtaɪə(r)/	a.	全部的；整个的；完全的
▲auspicious	/ɔːˈspɪʃəs/	a.	吉利的；吉祥的
*claw	/klɔː/	n.	（动物或禽类的）爪；（水生有壳动物的）钳
*ancestor	/ˈænsestə(r)/	n.	祖宗；祖先
*bubble	/ˈbʌbl/	v.	起泡，冒泡
▲broth	/brɒθ/	n.	（加入蔬菜的）肉汤，鱼汤
*dip	/dɪp/	v.	蘸；浸

💬 Phrases & expressions

be associated with	与……相关；与……联系
be regarded as	被认为是；被当作是；视为
sweep away	扫清；肃清；冲走
make way for	为……开路

生词数	生词率	*B级词汇	*A级词汇	▲四、六级词汇	超纲词汇
39	5.8%	15	15	6	3

Notes

Overseas Chinese or Sinophone populations 海外华人或华语语系人群

These countries include Singapore（新加坡）, Indonesia（印度尼西亚）, Malaysia（马来西亚）, Myanmar（缅甸）, Thailand（泰国）, Cambodia（柬埔寨）, the Philippines（菲律宾）, and Mauritius（毛里求斯）, as well as many in North America and Europe.

After-reading tasks

Task 1 Answer the following questions with the understanding of Reading B.

1. What time does the Chinese New Year begin in a year?

2. Why is food a very important part of the New Year celebrations?

3. What is the symbolic meaning of the fish?

4. Why is *Niangao* a must for Chinese New Year?

5. What is your favorite food for Chinese New Year?

Task 2 Translate the following paragraph into Chinese.

   Chinese New Year is associated with several myths and customs. The evening preceding Chinese New Year's Day is frequently regarded as an occasion for Chinese families to gather for the annual reunion dinner. It is also traditional for every family to thoroughly clean their house, in order to sweep away any ill-fortune and to make way for incoming good luck. Another custom is the decoration of windows and doors with red paper-cuts and couplets. Other activities include lighting firecrackers and giving money in red paper envelopes.

Unit 1 | Chinese Cuisine and Food Culture   17

Comprehensive exercises

Task 1 Match each term in Column A to the respective definition in Column B.

Column A   Column B

(   ) 1. bake   A. in water or another liquid at 100℃
(   ) 2. boil   B. in water or another liquid at a little less than 100℃
(   ) 3. fry   C. in the water or another liquid at 100℃ slowly and for a long time (e.g. beef)
(   ) 4. grill   D. in steam
(   ) 5. poach   E. in the oven, with very little or no oil (e.g. bread)
(   ) 6. roast   F. in the oven, with fat (e.g. meat)
(   ) 7. sauté   G. under (or over) direct heat (e.g. steak)
(   ) 8. steam   H. in fat or oil
(   ) 9. stew   I. in a little oil, for a short time

Task 2 Fill in the blanks with the words or expressions from Reading A and Reading B that match the meanings in the column on the right. The first letter of each word is given.

1. i_____   the power to have an effect on the way someone or something develops, behave, or thinks without using direct force or commands
2. a_____   to prevent something bad from happening
3. p_____   a thing or things that are owned by somebody
4. e_____   equal in value, amount, meaning, purpose, importance, etc.
5. c_____   to use something, especially fuel, energy, time, etc.
6. s_____   having an important or noticeable effect, or a particular meaning
7. r_____   to be a symbol of something
8. c_____   something is made of when it contains a number of part or things
9. i_____ _____   adding another fact to what has already been mentioned
10. b_____ _____   to be connected with something in some way

Task 3 Complete the following sentences with the words and expressions from Task 1. Change the form if necessary.

1. The simplest house _____ a single room with a sink in the corner and a toilet behind a partition.
2. You might be able to work from home some of the time, which would let you _____ wasted hours commuting back and forth.
3. Net exports _____ the difference between how much we export and import.
4. How much does TV advertising really _____ what people buy?
5. The question is how much junk food you _____ during the typical week.
6. He had been rich all his life, but he never much delight in the _____ he possessed.
7. Weibo is often said to be China's _____ to Twitter, but in some key ways it's different.
8. Event of the control must _____ the event handler method shown in the example.
9. _____ a small number of the company's brand will give users the impression, most brands do not take root in the hearts of users.
10. The White House did not disclose the contents of the call, but analysts said the timing was _____.

Task 4 Comment on the food or drink by choosing one suitable word for each answer.

| spicy | strong | sweet | hot | cooked |

Model: How is the chicken?
 I'm afraid it's not *spicy* enough for me.

1. How are you enjoying your longevity noodle soup?

_____

2. Is the curry (咖喱) all right for you?

_____

3. Is the black coffee all right, sir?

_____

4. How is the fish?

_____

5. Is that tea OK for you, honey?

_____

Task 5 Translate the following sentences into English, using the given words or phrases.

1. 中国菜分成八大菜系。
   (be divided into, cuisine)

2. 我们餐厅有很多素菜可供您选择。
   (vegetarian, choice)

3. 中餐礼仪是中华餐饮文化的重要组成部分。
   (table manner, Chinese diet culture)

4. 为什么中国厨师要花大量的时间练习刀工。
   (cook, cutting)

5. 如果您是招待贵宾，我建议点这道菜。这是我们的招牌菜。
   (entertain, house specialty)

Applied writing

Résumé (简历)

写简历是求职的必要环节，通常是为了获得面试机会。简历的内容一般包含个人简介、目标职位、教育背景、工作经验等信息。一份好的简历应简洁明了、信息真实准确，没有语法和拼写错误。

Sample

Résumé

Name: Xiao Yue   Position applied for: English teacher

	ENGLISH NAME	Moon	AGE	21
BASIC INFORMATION	GENDER	Female	HEIGHT(cm)	165cm
	DATE OF BIRTH	1993.5.17	WEIGHT(kg)	48kg
	PLACE OF BIRTH	Chengdu, Sichuan Province	NATIONALITY	Han
	CELLPHONE	15283119963	MARITAL STATUS	Single
EDUCATION BACKGROUND	NAME OF SCHOOL / COLLEGE / UNIVERSITY		FROM (Month/Year) TO (Month/Year)	MAJOR
	Chengdu Middle School		2008.09—2011.06	None
	Sichuan University		2011.09—2015.06	English
HOBBIES	travelling, playing billiards and reading			
REWARDS	2012 The First-prize Scholarship 2013 Excellent Student of Sichuan University 2014 National Scholarship			
WORKING EXPERIENCE	WORKING EXPERIENCE		PERIOD	POSITION
	Chengdu Xinhua Training School		2013.07—2013.09	Teaching assistant
	New Oriental School		2013.09—2014.03	English teacher
SELF REMARK	open-minded; optimistic; hard-working; good at teamwork			

Writing task

ABC Travel Agency put an advertisement on the local newspaper dated May 22nd, 2021, and a full-time tour guide is wanted. As a graduate majoring in Tourism Management, you are going to write a résumé to the Personnel Department of the travel agency.

Project performing

Employee recruitment

The personnel management of enterprises is to let the right people do the right things. Therefore, it is necessary to consider the establishment of enterprise management system, clear job responsibilities, and recruitment of employees suitable for job needs. According to job responsibilities, it's important for employers to hire employees with relevant professional skills and work enthusiasm.

Interview questions for reference:
- Where did you work? What is the specific work?
- Why do you want to work with our company?
- What position do you want to apply for?
- What kind of advantages and disadvantages do you think you have?
- What do you do in your spare time? Do you have any hobbies?
- How would you react if someone treated you badly at work?
- …

Please follow the task description to complete the project.

Step 1: Organize a small group of 4 to 6 students in your class;

Step 2: Discuss in groups, each group assumes the company type and the position that needs to be recruited;

Step 3: Each group gives a presentation to introduce the company, the position that needs to be recruited, as well as the basic qualities and job responsibilities required for the recruitment position;

Step 4: Role-play according to the suggested recruitment process and complete the dialogue in English.

Grammar

Inverted sentence (倒装句)

在英语中，主语和谓语有两种顺序：一是主语在前，这和汉语是一致的，称为自然语序（Natural order），反之，如果谓语在主语前面，就是倒装语序（Inverted order）。倒装又分为部分倒装（Partial inversion）和完全倒装（Full inversion）。

1. 部分倒装

（1）具有否定意义的词或短语，如never, little, hardly, seldom, no sooner, not until, not only, in no case等位于句首时，句子需用部分倒装，即助动词、情态动词或be动词放在主语之前。

Never have I seen such a performance.
我从未见过这样的表演。
Little does he know about America.
他对美国知之甚少。
Not until he finished his homework did he go home.
直到完成家庭作业他才回家。
Hardly had she gone out when a student came to visit her.
她刚出门，就有一个学生来看她。
In no case will he give up his dream.
在任何情况下他都不会放弃他的梦想。

（2）so... that...句型中so及其所修饰的部分位于句首时，句子需用部分倒装，即助动词、情态动词或be动词放在主语之前。

She is so beautiful that we all like her.
→So beautiful is she that we all like her.
她很漂亮，我们都喜欢她。
The teacher spoke so quickly that I couldn't follow her.
→So quickly did the teacher speak that I couldn't follow her.
老师讲得太快了，我听不懂。

He can express himself so well in English that everyone admires him.

→So well can he express himself in English that everyone admires him.

他能用英语很好地表达自己，每个人都钦佩他。

（3）"Only +状语（副词、介词短语或状语从句）"位于句首时，句子需用部分倒装，即助动词、情态动词或be动词放在主语之前。

Only then did he realize the importance of learning English.

直到那时他才意识到学习英语的重要性。

Only in this way can we keep fit.

只有这样我们才能保持健康。

Only when he took off his sunglasses did I recognize him.

直到他摘下墨镜我才认出他。

（4）so（也）, neither（也不）, nor（也不）位于句首时，句子需用部分倒装，即助动词、情态动词或be动词放在主语之前。

—He can speak English fluently.

—So can I.

—他能说一口流利的英语。

—我也可以。

—He will become a doctor next week.

—So will I.

—下周他将成为一名医生。

—我也会的。

—He isn't good at expressing himself.

—Neither/Nor do I.

—他不善于表达自己。

—我也一样。

—He didn't have a good time yesterday.

—Neither/Nor did I.

—他昨天玩得不开心。

—我也是。

2. 完全倒装

（1）here, there, now, then等副词位于句首，谓语动词常用be, come, go, lie, run，句子需用完全倒装，即谓语放在主语前面。

There goes the bell.
铃响了。

Here is your letter.
这是你的信。

Then came the chairman.
然后主席来了。

Now comes your turn.
现在轮到你了。

（2）表示运动方向的副词或地点状语位于句首，谓语表示运动的动词，句子需用完全倒装，即谓语放在主语前面。

Out rushed the children.
孩子们冲了出来。

Ahead sat an old woman.
前面坐着一位老妇人。

In came the teacher.
老师进来了。

注意：上述全部倒装的句型结构的主语必须是名词，如果主语是人称代词则不能完全倒装。

Away they went.
他们走了。

In he came.
他走了进来。

Out they rushed.
他们冲了出来。

（3）介词短语位于句首，句子需用完全倒装，即谓语放在主语前面。

Behind our school lies a river.
我们学校后面有一条河。

In front of the house sits a dog.
房子前面坐着一只狗。

At the foot of the mountain stands an old temple.
山脚下矗立着一座古庙。

Task 1 Choose the best answer to complete the sentences.

1. —Where is Kate?
   —Look, _____, she is at the school gate.
   A. there she is   B. there is she   C. here you are   D. here it is

2. _____, he knows a lot of things.
   A. A child as he is   B. Child as he is   C. A child as is he   D. Child as is he

3. Only when you realize the importance of foreign languages _____ them well.
   A. you can learn   B. can you learn   C. you learned   D. did you learn

4. Never before _____ seen such a stupid man.
   A. am I   B. was I   C. have I   D. shall I

5. Hardly _____ down _____ he stepped in.
   A. had I sat; than   B. I had sat; when   C. had I sat; then   D. had I sat; when

6. —You ought to have given them some advice.
   —_____, but who cared what I said?
   A. So ought you   B. So I ought   C. So did you   D. So I did

7. Only by practicing a few hours every day _____ be able to master the language.
   A. you can   B. can you   C. you will   D. will you

8. Not only _____ polluted but _____ crowded.
   A. was the city; were the street
   B. the city was; were the street
   C. was the city; the streets were
   D. the city was; the streets were

9. _____ reading and speaking English every day, he would speak it well enough now.
   A. Had he practiced   B. Did he practice   C. Should he practice   D. Were he to practice

10. Not until I began to work _____ how much time I had wasted.
    A. didn't I realize   B. did I realize   C. I didn't realize   D. I realize

Unit 1 | Chinese Cuisine and Food Culture

Task 2 Rewrite the sentences. Put the italic words at the beginning of the sentence and make necessary changes.

1. He had *no sooner* put down the receiver than the telephone rang again.

2. The enemy tried *in vain* to encircle and wipe out the guerrillas.

3. She was *so absorbed* in the work that she often forgot to take her meals.

4. Their fear was *such* that they didn't dare to turn off the light the whole night.

5. We must not relax our vigilance *under any circumstances*.

6. The enemy could *not* drag *a word of information* from him.

7. He *never* expected that the project would be completed so soon.

8. We should *not only* work hard ourselves, we should also get other people interested in the work.

9. He did *not* realize the seriousness of his mistake *until you talked with him*.

10. He has given me good advice *many a time*.

Self-evaluation

Rate your own progress in this unit.	D	M	P	F*
I learn many cookery words in English.	☐	☐	☐	☐
I get to know Chinese cuisine and its history.	☐	☐	☐	☐
I can talk about Chinese food culture.	☐	☐	☐	☐
I can write a résumé in English.	☐	☐	☐	☐
I have mastered the inverted sentence.	☐	☐	☐	☐

*Note: D (Distinction), M (Merit), P (Pass), F (Fail)

Unit 1 | Chinese Cuisine and Food Culture

Culture

 Task 1   Listen to the recording of *Chinese Cuisine History*, and then read the passage imitating the pronunciation and intonation of the last paragraph.

Chinese cuisine history

Chinese cuisine has a long history and is one of the Chinese cultural treasures. It is famous all over the world. Chinese cookery has developed and matured over the centuries, forming a rich cultural content. It is characterized by fine selection of ingredients, precise processing, particular care to the amount of fire, and substantial nourishment. Local flavors and snacks, and special dishes have formed according to regions, local products, climate, historical factors, and eating habits.

The two dominant philosophies of the Chinese culture are Confucianism and Taoism. Each influenced the course of Chinese history and the development of the culinary arts. Confucianism concerned itself with the art of cooking and placed great emphasis on the enjoyment of life. To the Chinese, food and friends are inseparable. A gathering without food is considered incomplete and improper.

Ever since the Shang and Zhou Dynasties, China's dietary culture has taken shape. By the Tang and Song Dynasties, the dining customs in the north and south developed respectively. People in the north liked salty food while those in the south liked sweet food.

During the Southern Song Dynasty (1127—1279 AD), the northerners moved to the south in large numbers. Gradually, the northern food culture influenced the south and formed its own style in the south. By the end of the Ming Dynasty, the Chinese cuisine was divided into Beijing style, Jiangsu style and Cantonese style. Beijing-style dishes were salty, and the Jiangsu-style and Cantonese-style dishes were sweet.

By the early Qing Dynasty, there existed four most influential cuisines: Shandong cuisine, Sichuan cuisine, Cantonese cuisine and Jiangsu cuisine.

Later, the dining habits of various parts of China developed considerably. Sichuan cuisine was further divided into Sichuan cuisine and Hunan cuisine. Cantonese cuisine was divided into Cantonese cuisine and Fujian cuisine. Jiangsu cuisine was divided into Jiangsu cuisine, Zhejiang cuisine and Anhui cuisine. By the late Qing Dynasty, Sichuan, Cantonese, Hunan, Shandong, Jiangsu, Zhejiang, Fujian, and Anhui cuisines gradually became the most influential and popular, finally forming "8 Chinese Cuisines".

Cuisine in China is a harmonious integration of color, flavor, taste, shape and the fineness of the instruments. For the cooking process, chefs pick various ingredients and seasonings while employing unparalleled complicated skills handed down from their fathers, ever aspiring to their ideal of perfection for all the senses. Among the many cooking methods they use are boiling, stewing, braising, frying, steaming, crisping, baking, and simmering and so on. When they finish their masterpieces they are arranged on a variety of plates and dishes so that they are a real pleasure to view, to smell and ultimately to savor.

Notes

1. **forming a rich cultural content** 形成了丰富的文化内涵
   中国饮食文化是在中国传统文化教育中的阴阳五行哲学思想、儒家伦理道德观念、中医养生学说，还有文化艺术成就、饮食审美风尚、民族性格特征诸多因素的影响下创造出来的。

2. **It is characterized by fine selection of ingredients, precise processing, particular care to the amount of fire, and substantial nourishment.** 它的特色就在于用料讲究，加工精细，善用火候和注重营养。

3. **Cuisine in China is a harmonious integration of color, flavor, taste, shape and the fineness of the instruments.** 中国烹饪是色、香、味、形和器的完美、和谐统一。

4. **For the cooking process, chefs pick various ingredients and seasonings while employing unparalleled complicated skills handed down from their fathers, ever aspiring to their ideal of perfection for all the senses.** 就烹饪的工序而言，厨师们精选各种配料和调味品，采用各自从他们的父辈传承下来的、无与伦比的复杂烹饪手艺，一直追求方方面面都能够做到完美。

5. **boiling, stewing, braising, frying, steaming, crisping, baking, and simmering**
   煮、炖、烧、炸、蒸、脆、烤、烘和煨

6. **…so that they are a real pleasure to view, to smell and ultimately to savor.**
   ……使它们既能赏心悦目，又美味可口，并且风味绝佳。

Task 2 Make discussions in groups on the following subjects.

1. Why does the speaker say that Chinese cuisine is one of the Chinese cultural treasures?
2. What are the typical characters of Chinese cuisines?
3. How are some Chinese dishes formed?
4. In ancient China, which philosophies influenced the development of Chinese culinary arts?
5. How many cooking methods do you know?

Unit 2

Workplace Etiquettes

Learning objectives

After studying this unit, you should be able to:
- have an in-depth understanding of workplace etiquette;
- enlarge your vocabulary related to office rules;
- write a thank-you letter in English;
- master how to use the nominal clause;
- keep good inter-personal relationships in the workplace.

Warm-up

Task 1 The following pictures are about some office rules. Match each picture with the accurate term in English.

(   ) **1.** Be on time   (   ) **2.** Use your indoor voice

(   ) **3.** Avoid office gossip   (   ) **4.** Treat email professionally

(   ) **5.** Share the credit   (   ) **6.** Stay home if you are sick

(   ) **7.** Keep phone usage to a minimum   (   ) **8.** Dress to make an impression

(   ) **9.** Be considerate in every way you can

Task 2 **Professional etiquette is essential if you want to get anywhere with your career. If you want to create a positive, lasting impression, you need to know what to say and how to act. Please finish the following quiz.**

1. A co-worker starts to tell you a story she heard about a co-worker's private life. You'd better _____.

   A. diplomatically tell her you're not interested in hearing it

   B. listen carefully. You figure that the more you know about your co-workers, the better equipped you'll be to navigate the politics in your office

   C. listen but share what you heard only at home and not in the office

2. A client has been waiting for you but you're running a little behind schedule. You need a few more minutes to finish what you're doing. You'd better _____.

   A. apologize in person and offer the client a cup of coffee and a magazine

   B. have someone else tell the client that you're running late and need a few more minutes

   C. keep the client waiting, but finish what you're working on as quickly as possible

3. One of your co-workers has too much to drink at your office's holiday party. You'd better _____.

   A. pull her aside and try to get her to switch to coffee or a soft drink

   B. take the drink out of her hand in front of everyone and make a joke of it

   C. ignore it

4. You have a non-urgent question for a co-worker who is talking with someone on the phone. You'd better _____.

   A. leave a note saying you need to speak with him and try to get him another time

   B. stand in the doorway and wait for him to get off the phone. You figure that that will save your time and that he's likely to be on the phone again when you come back later

   C. motion for him to put the caller on hold so you can speak to him

5. One of your co-workers tells you that the new employee in the office looks really sexy. You'd better _____.

   A. privately point out that the comment is sexist and offensive

   B. publicly criticize him for saying something sexist and offensive

   C. laugh heartily and voice your agreement. You figure that it's harmless fun

6. You notice that one of your male colleagues' fly is unzipped. You're a female and believe that he may be embarrassed if you point this out to him. You'd better _____.

   A. quietly and privately ask one of the other men in the office to tell him

   B. ignore it

   C. make a lighthearted joke of it

7. A co-worker made a dish that exploded in the office microwave and didn't clean up. You know who made the mess. You'd better _____.

   A. tell the person privately that the mess is still there and that it is courteous for her to clean it up so others can enjoy using the microwave

   B. ignore it

   C. leave a note anonymously on the microwave "Who Made This Mess?"

8. A client whose hearing is impaired wants to talk with you on the phone. You work in a cubicle. You'd better _____.

   A. remove yourself to a room where you can close the door so you can speak to the client at the volume he needs to hear you

   B. speak at a normal volume into the phone and figure that if the client can't hear you he can email you or come in person to talk with you

   C. raise your voice volume so that the client can hear you, even though everyone in and around you will hear what you're saying

> YOUR SCORE:
>
> A is worth 2 points, B is worth 1, and C is worth 0. If you scored 14—16 points, your business etiquette skills are strong. You're able to handle challenging situations courteously.
>
> If you scored 10—12 points, you usually practice good business etiquette. Seek ways to approach every situation in your workplace with respect and consideration for others.
>
> If you scored below 10 points, you would benefit from doing some additional work to improve your business etiquette skills. Look for books, courses, and one-on-one coaching to help you develop the manners you need in your workplace.

Reading A

Pre-reading questions

1. What matters in a workplace?
2. How should you make sure you have a positive and successful experience in the workplace?

5 workplace etiquette tips every professional should know

Whether you are starting your first internship or have many years of professional experience under your belt, how you present yourself to others in the workplace matters. Setting a professional tone is crucial to building new relationships and ensuring you have a positive, successful experience in the workplace.

1. Make a good first impression

People often form impressions about others within seconds of meeting them, so it's important to ensure you present yourself as a professional. Be aware of your body language and how others may perceive it. A good rule of thumb is to stand straight, maintain eye contact, and smile! Make sure you know the workplace dress code and office policies ahead of time. Arrive on time and be prepared for important meetings.

2. Avoid gossip

How you treat people says a lot about you. Don't make value judgments on people's importance in the workplace or speak negatively about your co-workers, even if you find yourself frustrated over a certain situation. Be thoughtful about how you interact with your supervisor(s), peers, and subordinates as well.

3. Communication is key

Communication is an important part of workplace etiquette. It's sometimes not what you say, but how you say it that counts, so be mindful of how you communicate with your colleagues in meetings and one-on-one conversations. In regard to email, be sure your correspondence inside and outside of your workplace is written clearly and free of spelling errors. Remember, email is a permanent record of any conversation so never put anything in writing that you would say to someone's face.

4. Understand your work environment

The values, policies, and procedures of a workplace can be difficult to discern at first. If you are in a larger organization with a structured human resource division, you may have access to an HR Manager or in-house trainings to keep you informed of your organization's expectations. In a smaller workplace setting, some of that knowledge may come from observing others and asking questions of your colleagues when needed. Lastly, observing the atmosphere and actions of others can help you understand what's appropriate and what's not, and how to best navigate the workplace while maintaining your professionalism.

5. Be personable yet professional

Sharing information about your personal life is your choice, but be cautious when it comes to what you share; some colleagues may be more open than others and might choose to keep their personal life private as well. Similarly, you may want to limit personal calls, emails, and other non-work related tasks to after-work hours. Within your workspace, it's okay to add personal touches but remember that your colleagues will see the space and consider it a reflection of your professional self. Lastly, getting to know your colleagues is a good thing but always be respectful of others' space. If you need to discuss something with them, don't just walk in; knock or make your presence known, and always offer to schedule a meeting for later in the day if they are busy in the moment.

(505 words)

New words

▲etiquette	/ˈetɪkət/	n.	礼仪；(社会或行业中的)礼节；规矩
▲internship	/ˈɪntɜːnʃɪp/	n.	(学生或毕业生的)实习期
*crucial	/ˈkruːʃl/	a.	关键的
*positive	/ˈpɒzətɪv/	a.	积极乐观的
*impression	/ɪmˈpreʃn/	n.	印象；效果
*perceive	/pəˈsiːv/	v.	感知；将……理解为
*negatively	/ˈneɡətɪvli/	ad.	消极的；负面的
*frustrate	/frʌˈstreɪt/	v.	使沮丧
▲subordinate	/səˈbɔːdɪnət/	n.	下级；部属
*correspondence	/ˌkɒrəˈspɒndəns/	n.	通信；相似
*error	/ˈerə(r)/	n.	错误；差错；谬误
*permanent	/ˈpɜːmənənt/	a.	永久的；永恒的
▲policy	/ˈpɒləsi/	n.	政策；方针
discern	/dɪˈsɜːn/	v.	辨别；了解
*division	/dɪˈvɪʒn/	n.	部门；分开
▲navigate	/ˈnævɪɡeɪt/	v.	导航；找到正确方法
▲professionalism	/prəˈfeʃənəlɪzəm/	n.	专业水平；专业素质
*cautious	/ˈkɔːʃəs/	a.	小心的；谨慎的
*reflection	/rɪˈflekʃn/	n.	反射；显示；表达
*presence	/ˈprezns/	n.	存在；出现
*schedule	/ˈʃedjuːl/	v.	安排；为……安排时间

Phrases & expressions

under one's belt	已有的经验和阅历（俚语）
present oneself	展现自我
be aware of	意识到，知道
make sure	确保，确信
dress code	着装要求
interact with	互动
be mindful of	注意，留心
in regard to	至于，关于
be respectful of	尊重他人

生词数	生词率	*B级词汇	*A级词汇	▲四、六级词汇	超纲词汇
21	4.2%	6	7	7	1

Notes

1. **A good rule of thumb is to stand straight, maintain eye contact, and smile!**
   一个好的经验法则（建议）是站直，保持眼神交流，并微笑！
   to stand straight...是动词不定式短语做表语。

2. **Be thoughtful about how you interact with your supervisor(s), peers, and subordinates as well.**
   要考虑好如何与你的上司、同事和下属交流。
   how you interact with...是由how引导的宾语从句，做介词about的宾语；and... as well意为"及；也"。

3. **It's sometimes not what you say, but how you say it that counts, so be mindful of how you communicate with your colleagues in meetings and one-on-one conversations.**
   有时候重要的不是你说了什么，而是你怎么说，所以要注意在会议和一对一的谈话中如何与同事交流。
   本句为强调句，其结构是"It's +被强调部分+that..."; not... but意为"不是……而是……"。

4. **If you are in a larger organization with a structured human resource division, you may have access to an HR Manager or in-house trainings to keep you informed of your organization's expectations.**
   如果你在一家较大的公司，人力资源部门结构合理，你可以通过人力资源经理或内部培训了解公司对你的期望。
   with意为"拥有，具备"; keep sb. informed of sth. 意为"告知某人某事"。

5. **Sharing information about your personal life is your choice, but be cautious when it comes to what you share.**
   分享个人生活信息是你的选择，但分享内容时要谨慎。
   when it comes to意为"当提到；就……而论"。

6. **Lastly, getting to know your colleagues is a good thing but always be respectful of others' space.**
   最后，了解同事是一件好事，但一定要尊重他人的空间。
   getting to know your colleagues是动名词短语做主语。

After-reading tasks

Task 1 Answer the following questions according to Reading A and then discuss them with your classmates.

1. How should you make a good first impression?
2. What should you do to avoid gossip in workplace?
3. What should you do with the correspondence at work?
4. How can you get to know the work environment if you are in a small workplace?
5. Is it OK to share your personal life in workplace? How should you draw boundaries between personal life and the work?

Task 2 Complete the mind map with your understanding of Reading A.

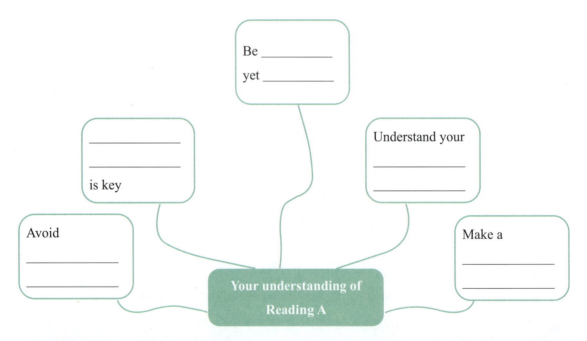

Unit 2 | Workplace Etiquettes 39

Listening and speaking

Task 1 Listen to Dialogue 1 and fill in the blanks.

Alex Jones: ___1___. My name is Alex Jones. I'm the new assistant in the office.

Miss Lee: ___2___. I heard you were coming today. Is today your first day here in the company?

Alex: Yes, ___3___ and getting started on my new job.

Miss Lee: First day is often exciting, isn't it? Here, ___4___. You can have this computer and telephone and share the copy machine with us in the office. ___5___?

Alex: This is wonderful. ___6___, Miss Lee.

Task 2 Listen to Dialogue 2 and fill in the blanks.

Helen: Mr. Jones, ___1___. I'm Mr. Windsor's assistant. Helen Brown. Please call me Helen.

Gerald: ___2___, Helen? Nice to meet you. And ___3___ me Gerald.

Helen: ___4___ to have you here for the meeting. How was your ___5___ to London?

Gerald: Fine, thanks. The train arrived on time with no ___6___.

Helen: That's great. Did you have any ___7___ finding us?

Gerald: Not at all. Your directions were very good.

Helen: Oh, thanks. So, could you please ___8___ and take a ___9___?

Gerald: The meeting room is on the second floor. ___10___ come this way?

Task 3 **Role-play in pairs according to the situation given below. The expressions given below are for your reference.**

Sophia works as a receptionist in a big company. Maria is the new colleague, and today is her first day in a new job.

- Good morning.
- Welcome to…
- My name is… Please call me…
- How is your trip to…?
- Is this your first trip to…?
- This is…, our sales/marketing/HR manager.
- Let me introduce you to…
- I'd like you to meet…
- I hope you enjoy your stay here.
- Thank you very much.
- You are so nice.

Task 4 **Listen to Dialogue 3 and number the sentences in the order you have heard.**

Maria Ramon:	Please have a seat, Mr. Saunders. I received your résumé a few weeks ago, and I must say I'm very impressed.
John Saunders:	Thank you.
Maria Ramon:	We're a small financial company, trading mostly stocks and bonds. ___1___
John Saunders:	Your company has an impressive reputation. And I've always wanted to work for a smaller company.
Maria Ramon:	That's good to hear! ___2___
John Saunders:	I'm a head broker in a large international company. I deal with clients on a daily basis, handling all aspects of their accounts personally.
Maria Ramon:	___3___
John Saunders:	I have a lot of experience in the stock market, and I enjoy working with people. As a matter of fact, in my current job I'm in charge of a team of eight brokers.
Maria Ramon:	Well, you might just be the person we've been looking for. ___4___
John Saunders:	Yes. ___5___
Maria Ramon:	You'd be working with two other head brokers. In other words, you'd be handling about a third of our clients.

(   ) A. Do you have any questions?

(   ) B. If I were hired, how many accounts would I be handling?

(   ) C. May I ask why you're interested in working for us?

(   ) D. Would you mind telling me a little bit about your present job?

(   ) E. Why do you think you are the right candidate for this position?

Unit 2 | Workplace Etiquettes

Task 5 Listen to the passage and fill in the blanks.

1. Many offices favor the _____ interior design.
2. There is less _____ in the modern office design.
3. The ability to focus on work becomes a problem if there is too much _____.
4. Being _____ of other people's beliefs is important.
5. If you are _____, it's better for everyone if you stay at home.

Task 6 Work in groups of three or four to have a discussion according to the scenarios.

Case scenarios for discussion

A.

Jane works as a cashier at a small grocery store. Her shift finishes at 3 p.m., but she can't leave until her co-worker, Anna, takes over from her. Anna is really nice and has been working at the grocery store for about 3 years, and Jane has been working there for the last 5 months. Recently, Anna is showing up later for work without any explanation and because of it, Jane is not able to leave until 3:10 p.m. This really upsets Jane and she has to rush to get to her computer classes. Anna has never explained or apologized for being late. Help Jane to solve this situation.

B.

Mark and Jack are co-workers at a drugstore. While they are working together stocking a shelf, they start talking about their work. They are not happy with their new superior and their new shifts. Mark tells Jack that he already started applying for other jobs and suggests that Jack do the same. But Jack says that his strategy is to ignore his new superior. As they talk, customers are passing by and listening to their conversation. Let's help Mark and Jack with workplace etiquette.

Reading B

Pre-reading questions

1. Do you know that business etiquette may differ considerably from country to country?
2. What problems can a person face not knowing the nuances of business etiquette?
3. What do you know about business etiquette in China and other countries?

Business etiquette tips

The success or failure of your business does not depend solely on your hard work and commitment. When you are trying to seal a big deal with an established player in your industry, it's often the nuances of business etiquette that can make or break your day. Business etiquette refers to a set of do's and don'ts when you are in a professional setting. In case you want to know about some business etiquette tips which can really help you earn the respect of fellow professionals, read on.

Tip#1: Attire

Business etiquette is not just about acceptable behavior but also what you wear. Always dress in good taste and make sure your clothes are not wrinkled. Other than that, you can wear suits, tuxedos (if it's a formal dinner) or business casual clothes according to what the occasion demands. Some formal events may require you to follow dress codes and so try not to deviate from those requirements.

Tip#2: Punctuality

In business, time is money. So make sure that you arrive at all appointments on time. Arriving a minute early is okay but being a minute late is not. Punctuality makes your associates understand your commitment to what you are doing. If you are hosting a meeting, make sure to arrive at least 30 minutes early and check on the arrangements.

Tip#3: The Handshake

One question that might be bothering you is when to shake hands. The simple answer to that would be to shake hands when you introduce yourself and then again when your meeting is over or you are leaving the premises. Greet everyone with a firm handshake coupled with a warm smile and direct eye contact. A limp handshake is a strict no-no. Also, when a group of guests are approaching you, wait for them to extend the hand. In case shaking hands is not possible, acknowledge people with a nod and a smile.

Tip #4: Introducing People

When you are introducing people to each other, you may find yourself in a bit of a fix about what the order of introduction should be. In that case, you should know that individuals who are lower down the organizational hierarchy should be introduced to those above them.

Tip #5: Speaking

When you are delivering a formal lecture, it is important to stand. Whether it's a stage or your board room, standing will help you draw the attention of the listeners and help them concentrate on what you are saying. Also remember to maintain eye contact, particularly if you are speaking to a small group of people. Do not use foul language or racial/sexist jokes when you are speaking.

Tip#6: Dining

When you are at a business party, never have more than two drinks. Getting tipsy can be really harmful for your image. You should also observe basic table manners such as keeping glass ware to the right and bread plates to the left. If you are the host, be sure to raise the first toast of the evening.

Follow these business etiquette tips and earn the respect of one and all.

(516 words)

New words

*considerably	/kənˈsɪdərəbli/	ad.	非常；很；相当多地
▲nuance	/ˈnuːɑːns/	n.	细微的差别
▲solely	/ˈsəʊlli/	ad.	唯一地
*commitment	/kəˈmɪtmənt/	n.	承诺
▲established	/ɪˈstæblɪʃt/	a.	已确立的
▲attire	/əˈtaɪə(r)/	n.	服装
*acceptable	/əkˈseptəbl/	a.	（社会上）认同的，认可的；可接受的
▲wrinkle	/ˈrɪŋkl/	n.	（尤指脸上的）皱纹
*suits	/suːts/	n.	西服；套装
▲tuxedo	/tʌkˈsiːdəʊ/	n.	燕尾服
*casual	/ˈkæʒuəl/	a.	随便的，非正式的
deviate	/ˈdiːvieɪt/	v.	偏离；违背
*requirement	/rɪˈkwaɪəmənt/	n.	要求；必要条件
*punctuality	/ˌpʌŋktjuˈælɪti/	n.	准时
*associate	/əˈsəʊsieɪt/	n.	同事；伙伴；合伙人
▲premise	/ˈpremɪs/	n.	（企业或机构使用的）房屋及土地；经营场所
▲limp	/lɪmp/	a.	无力的；柔软的
*approach	/əˈprəʊtʃ/	v.	靠近；接近
*acknowledge	/əkˈnɒlɪdʒ/	v.	承认；搭理
fix	/fɪks/	n.	（尤指由自己引起的）困境，窘境
*individual	/ˌɪndɪˈvɪdʒuəl/	n.	个人

*deliver	/dɪˈlɪvə/	v.	发表
*organizational	/ˌɔːɡənaɪˈzeɪʃənl/	a.	组织的；机构的
▲hierarchy	/ˈhaɪərɑːki/	n.	等级制度（尤指社会或组织）
▲foul	/faʊl/	a.	很令人不快的；下流的
▲racial	/ˈreɪʃl/	a.	种族的；种族间的；人种的
sexist	/ˈseksɪst/	n.	性别歧视者
▲tipsy	/ˈtɪpsi/	a.	略有醉意的
*observe	/əbˈzɜːv/	v.	注意到；观察到
*toast	/təʊst/	n.	敬酒；祝酒

Phrases & expressions

seal a deal	达成交易
refer to	查阅，提及
according to	根据
concentrate on	专注于
couple with	与……连接在一起；相伴随
in case	万一；假使

生词数	生词率	*B级词汇	*A级词汇	▲四、六级词汇	超纲词汇
30	5.8%	7	8	13	2

Notes

1. **When you are trying to seal a big deal with an established player in your industry, it's often the nuances of business etiquette that can make or break your day.**
   当你试图与行业内的知名企业达成一笔大交易时，往往是商业礼仪的细微差别决定了你这一天的成败。
   make a day 开心愉悦的一天；break a day 糟糕的一天。

2. **Other than that, you can wear suits, tuxedos (if it's a formal dinner) or business casual clothes according to what the occasion demands.**
   除此之外，你还可以根据场合需要穿西装、无尾晚礼服（如果是正式晚宴）或商务休闲装。
   other than 除了，除……以外；according to 根据。

3. **In that case you should know that individuals who are lower down the organizational hierarchy should be introduced to those above them.**
   在这种情况下，你应该知道，应该把职位较低的人介绍给职位高于他们的人。
   who are lower down... 为限制性定语从句修饰 individuals；lower than 职位低于。

4. **If you are the host, be sure to raise the first toast of the evening.**
   如果你是主人，一定要第一个祝酒。
   raise a toast/make a toast 祝酒。

Unit 2 | Workplace Etiquettes

After-reading tasks

Task 1 Answer the following questions with your understanding of Reading B.

1. Do you think dress code is important in workplace? Why?

2. Why is it important to be punctual?

3. What should a handshake be like?

4. Which should be introduced first, your boss to your client or your client to your boss?

5. Why is it important to stand while lecturing?

6. Is it appropriate to have alcohol at a business party?

7. Do you find these tips useful? Which of them are new to you and which have you already known? Can you give some other tips?

Task 2 Decide whether each of the following actions is right or wrong.

No.	Variants	Right(√)	Wrong(×)
1	If you introduce your client to your boss, you say _____. A. Mr. Brown, I'd like you to meet Mr. Booth, my boss B. Mr. Booth, I'd like you to meet our client, Mr. Brown		
2	If someone forgets to introduce you, you _____. A. move on with the conversation without saying anything B. say something like "My name is Bill Jones, I don't believe we've met"		
3	If you forget someone's name, you _____. A. admit it like this: "Your face is familiar, please help me with your name" B. keep talking without mentioning his or her name		
4	When shaking hands, _____. A. a woman extends her hand first B. it doesn't matter who extends the hand first, business etiquette is gender neutral		
5	When going through the door, _____. A. The host goes through the door first to be ready to direct the guest B. The guest goes through the door first; it's a common act of hospitality		
6	If your colleague's zipper is open, _____. A. it's OK to tell him in private B. it's not appropriate to mention it		
7	When having lunch together, _____. A. The host—the one who invites—pays for the lunch B. Both business colleagues pay half		
8	You are at a meeting and expecting an important call. _____. A. It's OK to leave your cell phone on if you've notified your colleagues B. Your cell phone should be turned off or adjusted to vibrate mode		
9	You've invited your business partner to a business lunch and upon arrival a maitre d' (餐厅领班) is waiting to escort you. You _____. A. go after the maitre d' and your partner follows you B. let your guest follow the maitre d' first		
10	When you receive someone else's business card, you should _____. A. look at the card and acknowledge it B. pass them your business card		

Comprehensive exercises

Task 1 Fill in the blanks with the words or phrases from Reading A and Reading B that match the meanings in the column on the right. The first letter of each word is given.

1. d_____   bargain, transaction, or agreement
2. t_____   dinner jacket
3. p_____   a place of business
4. f_____   dilemma
5. h_____   a system of person or things arranged in a graded order
6. f_____   offensive to the senses; revolting
7. s_____   plan for an activity or event
8. c_____   being careful; prudent
9. p_____   displaying affirmation or acceptance or certainty, etc.
10. s_____ a person who is lower in rank

Task 2 Fill in the blanks with the words given below in proper forms.

| perceive | frustrate | observe | navigate | cautious |
| acknowledge | positive | crucial | established | commitment |

1. UN officials privately _____ this is a big number that may be hard to fill.
2. I'll drive, and you can _____.
3. Students must _____ for themselves the relationship between success and effort.
4. Sainsbury's, like John Lewis, was _____ about how well it would continue to perform this year.
5. They require _____ and determination to stay the course because the road ahead is long.
6. This is a _____ step to renewing self-confidence and being entirely comfortable with who you are.
7. He wanted to _____ me on how I asked questions, how I interacted with the people.
8. Few things _____ me more than dealing with people who feel they are entitled.
9. These range from _____ companies to start-ups.
10. Her husband became much more _____ and was soon back in full-time employment.

Task 3 Rewrite the following sentences after the models.

Model 1: It's sometimes not what you say, but how you say it that counts.
→Sometimes, *what matters* is *not* what you say, *but* how you say it.

1. It's sometimes not what you say, but what you do that counts.

2. It's sometimes not where you go, but who you go with that counts.

Model 2: The values, policies, and procedures of a workplace can be difficult to discern at first.
→*It can be difficult to* discern the values, polices, and procedures of a workplace at first.

1. An original movie without subtitles can be hard to understand.

2. The benefits of regular exercises can be easy to see in a month.

Task 4 Translate the following sentences into English, using the given phrases.

1. 它们也可以指流行文化和新文化趋势。(refer to)

2. 请一定要接种疫苗。(make sure)

3. 关于你对我未来的职业选择的疑问，我下定决心要做一名口译员。(in regard to)

4. 我们需要集中在核心业务上。(concentrate on)

5. 如今由于技术的进步，人们互动的方式发生了很大的变化。(interact with)

Applied writing

Thank-you letter (感谢信)

　　感谢信是对收信人的某一行为表示感谢的信函，在日常和商务活动中使用的频率非常高，例如当前任老板给你写了推荐信，或是同事在项目中帮助了你，都应该表示感谢。感谢信通常带有浓厚的感情色彩，用于表达真挚的情感。具体写作步骤如下：

- Address the person appropriately. (开头称呼)
- Say thank you. (表达感谢)
- Give (some) specifics. (提供细节)
- Say thank you again. (再次表达感谢)
- Sign off (结尾写敬语及签名)

1. 信的开头，称呼要恰当。不熟悉的人可以用"Dear Mr. / Mrs.+姓"；熟悉的用"Dear +名"。
2. 首段直接表示感谢，表明写作目的，让对方感受到你的诚意。
3. 主体段落写明感谢的原因，要展开说明具体的理由、所介绍的具体事例等。
4. 在署名前使用恰当的结尾敬语，如"Best regards,"或"Sincerely,"。

Sample 1

Dear Mr. Smith,

　　I hope you are well. I just wanted to say thank you so much for writing me a letter of reference for the job at XYZ Company.

　　I really appreciate you taking the time to write the letter. I am happy to announce that I have a second interview with the company next week! I will let you know how it goes.

　　Again, thank you so much. I greatly appreciate your assistance with my job search.

Best regards,

Jason Jones

Sample 2

Dear Ms. Lee,

I would like to thank you for the invaluable support you provided to me during my recent career search.

When I began this search, I had very little idea how to go about it—or especially, how to network to discover new job opportunities. The information and advice you gave (in particular, the list of contacts you shared with me) made all the difference.

I'm happy to tell you that I have just accepted a new position with ACME Auto! I greatly appreciate your generosity. Thank you so much!

Sincerely,

Sarah Smith

Useful sentences in writing a thank-you letter

1. I am writing to express my thanks for... 我写这封信是为了表达我对……的感谢。
2. I would like to convey in this letter my heartfelt thanks to you for... 我想在这封信中表达我对……的衷心感谢。
3. Thank you so much for the gift you sent me. 非常感谢你送给我的礼物。
4. Many thanks for all good things you have done in helping us to... 非常感谢您为帮助我们……所做的一切。
5. I would like to take this opportunity to express my great appreciation for your timely help and assistance. 愿借此机会对您的及时帮助表示衷心的感谢。
6. Thanks again for your kind help/consideration. 再次感谢您的帮助（关怀）。
7. Thank you for your assistance with... 感谢您对……的帮助。
8. Thank you for your attention to this matter. 谢谢您对此事的关注。
9. Your support is greatly appreciated. 非常感谢您的支持。
10. I'd like to express my/our appreciation for... 我想对……表示我（们）的感谢。

Writing task

Write a thank-you letter according to the instructions given in Chinese.

请你写一封感谢信给杰克逊教授（Professor Jackson）。内容如下：感谢他在工作选择问题上给予了宝贵的意见，非常感谢他的指教。你之前在工作选择中存在困惑，按照他说的做了以后，收效甚佳。你选择了那份工作，并认为这是你所能做出的最明智的选择。

Words for reference

工作选择: career choice　　　　　　　　建议: advice/suggestion
收效甚佳: work well　　　　　　　　　明智的: wise/smart

Project performing

It's been said that "You never get a second chance to make a first impression." The first few minutes of your meeting with a client is the most important because first impressions last longer. Proper greetings create great first impressions and opportunities for memorable experiences for customers which will make them want to come back again. Here are six stages of greeting a visitor to your company.

- Stage 1: First greeting (打招呼)
- Stage 2: Introducing yourself and repeating the visitor's name (自我介绍，重复到访者的姓名)
- Stage 3: Making small talks with the visitor (和客人寒暄)
- Stage 4: Giving the visitor a visitor's card (给访客发放访客证)
- Stage 5: Showing the visitor the way to the meeting (为访客引路)
- Stage 6: Making the visitor feel comfortable before the meeting (让访客感受宾至如归)

Exercises

You are going to greet some visitors to your company's meeting. Work in groups and figure out what should be done in each stage. Get the job done in a professional and efficient way.

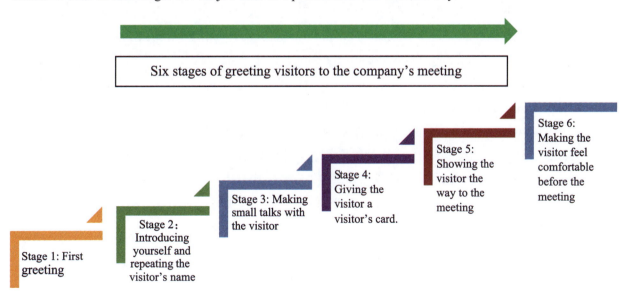

Grammar

Nominal clause (名词性从句)

名词性从句是在句子中起名词作用的句子，其功能相当于名词词组，在复合句中能担任主语、宾语、表语、同位语等。因此根据它在句中不同的语法功能，名词性从句可分为主语从句、宾语从句、表语从句和同位语从句。

1. 主语从句

主语从句通常由下列词引导：

（1）从属连词that, whether等。

Whether he can come to the party on time depends on the traffic.
他能否按时来参加聚会取决于交通情况。

（2）连接代词what, who, which, whatever, whoever, whom, whichever等。

What he wants to tell us is not clear. 他要跟我们说什么，还不清楚。

Who will win the match is still unknown. 谁能赢得这场比赛还不得而知。

（3）连接副词how, when, where, why等。

Where the English evening will be held has not yet been announced.
英语晚会将在哪里举行，还没有宣布。

2. 宾语从句

（1）由连接词that引导的宾语从句。

that引导宾语从句时，that在句中不担任任何成分，在口语或非正式的文体中常被省去。

He has told me (that) he will go to Shanghai tomorrow. 他已经告诉我他明天要去上海。

注意：在demand, order, suggest, decide, insist, desire, request, command, doubt等表示要求、命令、建议、决定等意义的动词后，宾语从句常用 "(should)+动词原形"。

I insist that she (should) do her work alone. 我坚持要她自己工作。

（2）由who, whom, which, whose, what, when, where, why, how, whoever, whatever, whichever等连接词引导的宾语从句相当于特殊疑问句，应注意句子语序要用陈述语序。

I want to know what he has told you. 我想知道他告诉了你什么。

She always thinks of how she can work well. 她总是在想怎样能把工作做好。

（3）whether与if表示"是否"时，在下列情况下一般只能用whether，不用if。

①引导主语从句在句首时，只能用whether。

Whether there is life on the moon is an interesting question.
月球上有没有生命是个有趣的问题。

②引导表语从句，只能用whether。

The question is whether we can get in touch with her. 问题是我们是否能联系上她。

③引导介词宾语时，只能用whether。

His father is worried about whether he lose his work. 他的父亲担心他是否会失去工作。

④后接动词不定式时，只能用whether。

Can you tell me whether to go or to stay? 你能否告诉我是去还是留？

⑤if与whether都可以与or not连用，但后面紧跟着or not时只能用whether。

We didn't know whether or not she was ready.（此时只能用whether）

我们不清楚她是否准备好了。

3. 同位语从句

同位语从句用于对其前面的名词进行解释说明，通常由that引导。可用于同位语从句的名词有advice, demand, doubt, fact, hope, idea, information, message, news, order, problem, promise, question, request, suggestion, truth, wish, word等。

The news that we won the game is exciting. 我们赢得这场比赛的消息令人激动。

I have no idea when he will come back home. 我不知道他什么时候回来。

Task 1 Fill in the blanks with the suitable conjunctions given below.

that	who	whose	what
why	if	whether	

1. _____ will be the new manager is still unknown.
2. I'm thinking about _____ I should quit my present job.
3. You'll be surprised to learn _____ name I've found on the list.
4. You should have guessed _____ she would surely let you down even at the most unexpected occasions.
5. It's not difficult to understand _____ different people speak different languages.
6. People, at times, can be so blind that they don't even see _____ is in front of their eyes.

Task 2 Choose the best answer to complete the sentences.

1. Does anybody know _____ on the ground?
   A. how long this plane will be   B. how long will be this plane
   C. how long will this plane be   D. that how long this plane will be

2. —This restaurant is very expensive!
   —It is, but order _____ want. This is a very special occasion.
   A. what is it you   B. what do you   C. whatever you   D. whatever you did

3. —What did your grammar teacher want to talk to you about?
   —I did badly on the last test. She _____ study for it.
   A. said why didn't I   B. asked why I didn't   C. said why I didn't   D. asked why didn't I

4. I talked to Bob two weeks ago. I thought he wanted to know about my cat, but I misunderstood him. He asked me where _____, not my cat.
   A. is my hat   B. my hat was   C. my hat is   D. was my hat

5. —I can't decide what color I want for my bedroom. What do you think?
   —You should choose _____ color you want. You're the one who will have to live with it.
   A. whichever that   B. whatever   C. however that   D. that what

6. Did you remember to tell Mark _____ he should bring to the meeting tomorrow?
   A. that   B. what   C. if   D. that what

7. —Let's go to the Riverton this weekend.
   —Sounds like fun. Could you tell me _____ from here?
   A. how far is it   B. how far it is   C. it how far is   D. how far is

8. —This cake is terrible. What happened?
   —It's my grandmother's recipe, but she forgot to tell me how long _____ it.
   A. I should bake   B. should I bake   C. do I bake   D. to bake

9. Tom walked into the huge hall to register for classes. At first, he simply looked around and wondered what _____ supposed to do.
   A. was she   B. am I   C. he was   D. I am

10. Edward's interview was very intense (紧张). The interviewer wanted to know many facts about his personal life, and even asked him _____ had ever used any illegal drugs of any kind.
    A. that if he   B. that he   C. if or not he   D. whether or not he

Self-evaluation

Rate your own progress in this unit.	D	M	P	F*
I can tell others how to present myself well in a workplace.	☐	☐	☐	☐
I can take the right actions concerning business etiquette.	☐	☐	☐	☐
I can follow the correct steps in greeting visitors to our company.	☐	☐	☐	☐
I can tell others the new office etiquette of post-COVID-19.	☐	☐	☐	☐
I can write a thank-you letter in English.	☐	☐	☐	☐
I have mastered the nominal clause.	☐	☐	☐	☐

*Note: D (Distinction), M (Merit), P (Pass), F (Fail)

Culture

Welcome back to office

COVID-19 has greatly changed the way people live, the way they work and the way they interact with each other. After the pandemic, it sounds like a treat coming back to your desk at the office. Now it feels like something bigger: a sign that life is finding its way back to what it was once before, at least somewhat.

Task 1 Watch the video, then fill in the missing information.

Thomas and Henry

Thomas: Henry

Henry: Thomas, ___1___ . So, ___2___ from home?

Thomas: Yeah, it was good. Got some. ___3___ to spend with. ___4___ .

Henry: So, it's ___5___ , uh.

Thomas: Yeah.

Thomas and Meredith

Meredith: Hey, Thomas.

Thomas: Better make a second one for the boss here first. I'm sure she ___6___ .

Meredith: ___7___ . Just didn't have the same resource ___8___ .

Meredith and Henry

Henry: Meredith.

Meredith: Hey, Henry. ___9___ ?

Henry: ___10___ .

Meredith: ___11___ the help with the IT stuff. I know it's not exactly in your job description.

Henry: Don't worry, Meredith. Always ___12___ .

Meredith: Welcome back to the office.

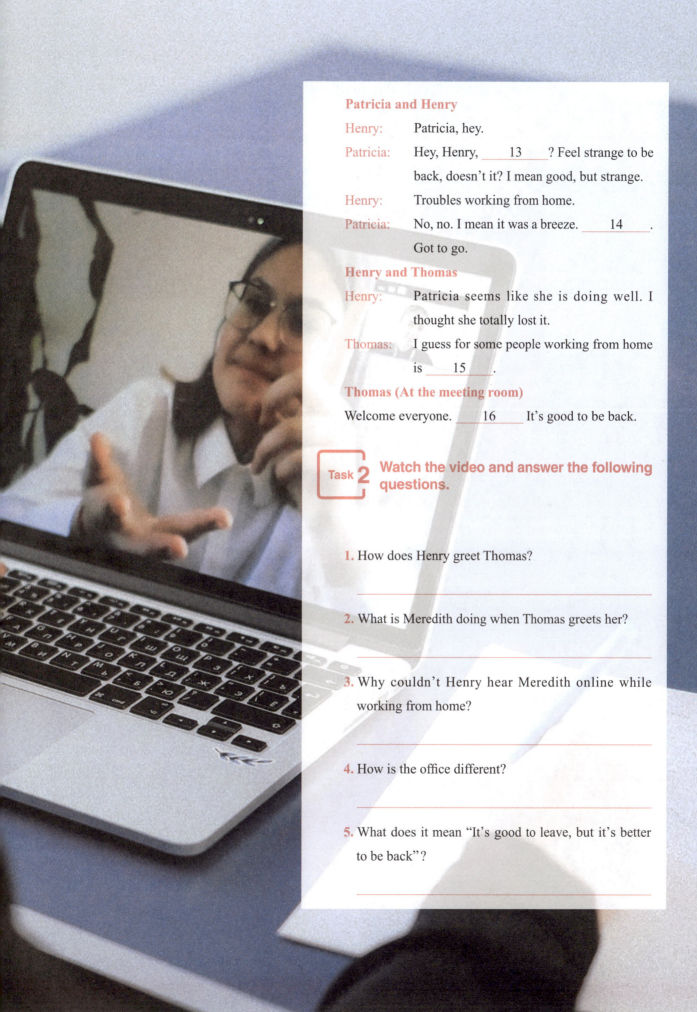

Patricia and Henry

Henry: Patricia, hey.

Patricia: Hey, Henry, ___13___? Feel strange to be back, doesn't it? I mean good, but strange.

Henry: Troubles working from home.

Patricia: No, no. I mean it was a breeze. ___14___. Got to go.

Henry and Thomas

Henry: Patricia seems like she is doing well. I thought she totally lost it.

Thomas: I guess for some people working from home is ___15___.

Thomas (At the meeting room)

Welcome everyone. ___16___ It's good to be back.

Task 2 Watch the video and answer the following questions.

1. How does Henry greet Thomas?
   _____

2. What is Meredith doing when Thomas greets her?
   _____

3. Why couldn't Henry hear Meredith online while working from home?
   _____

4. How is the office different?
   _____

5. What does it mean "It's good to leave, but it's better to be back"?
   _____

Unit 3

Intangible Cultural Heritage and Regional Development

Learning objectives

After studying this unit, you should be able to:
- read the article about intangible cultural heritage;
- enlarge your vocabulary related to intangible cultural heritage;
- understand the reading passage "The Living Heritage and the COVID-19 pandemic";
- get to know intangible cultural heritage & regional development in China;
- write letters of invitation in English;
- master how to use the predicative clause.

Warm-up

Task 1 The following pictures are about some intangible cultural heritages in China. Match each picture to the accurate name in English.

(   ) 1. Chinese calligraphy
(   ) 2. shadow play
(   ) 3. 24 Solar Terms
(   ) 4. Kun Opera
(   ) 5. Dragon Boat Festival
(   ) 6. acupuncture
(   ) 7. Tai Chi
(   ) 8. paper cutting
(   ) 9. calculation with an abacus

Task 2 The following is a video clip from CCTV, in which "24 Solar Terms", is listed as intangible cultural heritage from China in 2016. Watch the video and answer the following questions.

1. How long is the "24 Solar Terms"?
   _____
   _____

2. What was the "24 Solar Terms" created for?
   _____
   _____

3. Where was it initially developed?
   _____
   _____

4. How do the terms influence neighboring people's lives?
   _____
   _____

Reading A

Pre-reading questions

What is an intangible cultural heritage?

What is an intangible cultural heritage

The intangible cultural heritage is the expression, representation, skill, and practices which individuals, groups, and communities recognize as their cultural heritage. These include all the processes and products of a specific custom which are preserved and passed down from one generation to the other. Some of these heritages are intangible including festivals, crafts, cuisine, skills, music and even songs while others are tangible artifacts. These cultures cannot be stored in the museum, but we can only experience them through the cultural vehicles (defined as human treasures by the United Nations) who express them.

The groups and communities recreate intangible heritage in response to their surroundings. Their interaction with their history and nature grants them a sense of stability and uniqueness, therefore, promoting the admiration of cultural diversity and creativity. The living heritage is the cultural diversity of humanity and preserving it assures guaranteed continuity of creativity.

What are the different types of intangible cultural heritage?

1. Food heritage

As sustainable development gains momentum, various food-related nominations have been submitted to the convention list of intangible cultural heritage that needs to be preserved. Some of these diets include Japanese washoku dietary culture, traditional Mexican cuisine, and the Mediterranean cuisine.

2. Oral history

Living heritage is entirely different from the verbal history discipline especially when it comes to the interpretation, preservation, and recording of historical information based on personal opinions and experience of the speaker. The intangible cultural heritage tries to preserve living heritage by merely guarding the processes which make it possible for the shared knowledge and traditions to be passed to the next generations while oral history collects all the historical detail and then preserve them.

3. Dance heritage

The list also included a variety of dance genre associated with celebrations, singing, and music from every

corner of the world. It contains various ritual and celebratory dances like Ugandan Ma'di bowl lyre dance and music and some social dances like Rumba. Other dance-moves recognized as the heritage from certain nations but practiced globally include Tango and Flamenco. These routines are sophisticated heritages which involve numerous artifacts, traditions, culture and music which results in some intangible and tangible elements thus making it a unique type of heritage to preserve.

UNESCO introduced their convention for preserving the living cultures in 2003 which took effect on April 20, 2006. It recommended that all the members create an inventory of the intangible culture heritage within their territories and work with the people maintaining these cultures to ensure that they are preserved. It also provided some funds which can be collected by any of their members and be used to support the maintenance of these living cultures.

(442 words)

New words

intangible	/ɪnˈtændʒəbl/	a.	无形的
▲representation	/ˌreprɪzenˈteɪʃn/	n.	表现
*process	/ˈprəʊses/	n.	过程；进程
*preserve	/prɪˈzɜːv/	v.	保存，保留
▲craft	/krɑːft/	n.	手艺；工艺
*cuisine	/kwɪˈziːn/	n.	烹饪；风味
artifact	/ˈɑːtɪfækt/	n.	手工制品，手工艺品
*vehicle	/ˈviːəkl/	n.	手段，工具
recreate	/ˌriːkriˈeɪt/	v.	再现；再创造
▲surroundings	/səˈraʊndɪŋz/	n.	周围的环境
▲grant	/grɑːnt/	v.	准予，允许
▲stability	/stəˈbɪləti/	n.	稳定性
*unique	/juˈniːk/	a.	唯一的；独特的
▲admiration	/ˌædməˈreɪʃn/	n.	钦佩
diversity	/daɪˈvɜːsəti/	n.	多样化
*guarantee	/ˌɡærənˈtiː/	v.	保证；担保
continuity	/ˌkɒntɪˈnjuːəti/	n.	连续性；持续性
sustainable	/səˈsteɪnəbl/	a.	可持续的
momentum	/məˈmentəm/	n.	动力；势头
nomination	/ˌnɒmɪˈneɪʃn/	n.	提名；推荐

*oral	/ˈɔːrəl/	a.	口头的
▲interpretation	/ɪnˌtɜːprəˈteɪʃn/	n.	理解；解释
genre	/ˈʒɒnrə/	n.	（文学、艺术、电影或音乐的）体裁，类型
*celebration	/ˌselɪˈbreɪʃn/	n.	庆典；庆祝
ritual	/ˈrɪtʃuəl/	a.	庆典的
▲sophisticated	/səˈfɪstɪkeɪtɪd/	a.	复杂的；水平高的
inventory	/ˈɪnvəntri/	n.	库存
▲territory	/ˈterətri/	n.	领土；版图
▲maintain	/meɪnˈteɪn/	v.	维持；保持

💬 Phrases & expressions

recognize as	承认
pass down	传递，传承
define as	界定；定义为
in response to	作为回应
interaction with	与……相互作用
submit to	呈交
based on	在……基础上
a variety of	各种各样的
associated with	与……有关
result in	导致
take effect	生效

📖 Proper names

intangible cultural heritage	非物质文化遗产
the United Nations	联合国
the Mediterranean diet	地中海式饮食
Ugandan Ma'di bowl lyre dance	乌干达音乐舞蹈
Rumba	伦巴舞（源自古巴的一种快步舞）；伦巴舞曲
Tango	探戈舞；探戈舞曲
Flamenco	弗拉明戈舞；弗拉明戈吉他舞曲

生词数	生词率	*B级词汇	*A级词汇	▲四、六级词汇	超纲词汇
29	6.6%	3	5	10	11

📂 Notes

1. The intangible cultural heritage is the expression, representation, skill, and practices which

Unit 3 | Intangible Cultural Heritage and Regional Development

individuals, groups, and communities recognize as their cultural heritage.

非物质文化遗产是个人、团体和社区承认为其文化遗产的表达、表现、技能和实践。

which 引导的定语从句修饰先行词 expression, representation, skill and practices。

2. Some of these heritages are intangible including festivals, crafts, cuisine, skills, music and even songs while others are tangible artifacts.

其中一些遗产是无形的，包括节日、手工艺、美食、技能、音乐甚至歌曲，而另一些则是有形的文物。

此句中 while 作并列连词用，意为"而，然而"，表对比。

3. Living heritage is entirely different from the verbal history discipline especially when it comes to the interpretation, preservation, and recording of historical information based on personal opinions and experience of the speaker.

活态文化遗产与口头历史学科完全不同，尤其是在基于说话人个人观点和经验的历史信息的解释、保存和记录方面。

when it comes to 意为"说到；当谈到；一谈到；当提到"。

4. These routines are sophisticated heritages which involve numerous artifacts, traditions, culture and music which results in some intangible and tangible elements thus making it a unique type of heritage to preserve.

这些动作是复杂的遗产，涉及许多文物、传统、文化和音乐，产生了一些无形和有形的元素，从而使其成为一种独特的遗产类型。

现在分词 making 引导结果状语。

5. It recommended that all the members create an inventory of the intangible culture heritage within their territories and work with the people maintaining these cultures to ensure that they are preserved.

它（联合国教科文组织）建议所有成员在其领土内建立一份非物质文化遗产清单，并与维护这些文化的人合作，以确保这些文化得到保护。

当主句的谓语动词为 insist, order, command, suggest, advise, recommend, ask, demand, require, request 等时，其后的宾语从句要使用虚拟语气"(should)+动词原形"结构。

After-reading tasks

Task 1 Read the sentences below and decide whether they are true or false according to Reading A.

( ) 1. Festivals, crafts, cuisine, skills, music and even songs are tangible artifacts.

( ) 2. The intangible cultural heritage cannot be stored in the museum, but we can only experience them through the cultural vehicles who express them.

( ) 3. Japanese washoku dietary culture, traditional Chinese cuisine, and the Mediterranean cuisine are diets in the convention list of intangible cultural heritage.

( ) 4. The dance heritage contains Ugandan Ma'di bowl lyre dance, Rumba, Tango and Flamenco.

( ) 5. UNESCO introduced their convention for preserving the living cultures in 2003 which took effect on April 20, 2006.

Task 2 Complete the mind map below with the understanding of Reading A.

Intangible cultural heritage

the definition of ICH	the ___1___ and practices which individuals, groups, and communities recognize as their cultural heritage. These include all the ___2___ which are preserved and passed down from one generation to the other.
intangible heritage & tangible heritage	Some of these heritages are intangible including ___3___ and even songs. Others are tangible artifacts, buildings, cultural relics and sites.
the different types of ICH	___4___ Heritage, e.g. Japanese washoku dietary culture, traditional Mexican cuisine, and the Mediterranean cuisine. Oral History: collects all the ___5___ and then preserve them. Dance Heritage: a variety of ___6___ associated with celebrations, singing, and music from every corner of the world. e.g. Ugandan Ma'di bowl lyre dance, ___7___.
the function of UNESCO in ICH	UNESCO ___8___ for preserving the living cultures in 2003. It recommended that all the members create an inventory of the ___9___ within their territories. It also ___10___ which can be collected by any of their members and be used to support the maintenance of these living cultures.

Unit 3 | Intangible Cultural Heritage and Regional Development

Listening and speaking

Task 1 Listen to the dialogue and choose the best answer.

1. What does the woman think about climate change?
    A. It seems a depressing topic.
    B. It has little impact on our daily life.
    C. It sounds quite alarming.
    D. It is getting more serious these days.

2. What's the genre of *Carmen*?
    A. A Spanish love story.   B. A Spanish comedy.
    C. A British tragedy.   D. A British comedy.

3. Why do the speakers give up going to the Spanish dance festival tonight?
    A. The man doesn't understand Spanish.
    B. The woman doesn't really like dancing.
    C. They don't want something too noisy.
    D. They can't make it to the theatre in time.

4. What does the critic say about the comedy performed in the city theater?
    A. It would be more fun without Mr. Whitehead hosting.
    B. It has too many acts to hold the audience's attention.
    C. It is the most amusing show he has ever watched.
    D. It is a show inappropriate for a night of charity.

5. What does the woman decide to do tomorrow?
    A. Watch a comedy.   B. Go and see the dance.
    C. Book the tickets online.   D. See a film with the man.

Task 2 Listen to the news report and match the following choices in the order you have heard.

And more evidence on how good ___1___, a new study reveals why and how it may help you live longer, ABC's Reena has the details.

This morning a diet known for trimming your waistline might also be adding to your life expectancy, a new study says that ___2___ by extending a part of your DNA called telomeres, telomeres are the caps on the end of all chromosomes, often compare to the ends of shoe laces, and their leg is a marker of aging, as we age they get shorter, but according to the study ___3___, helping to prevent aging from taking its toll on cells, researchers followed nearly 5,000 nurses in a long term study and say those ___4___ ended up with longer telomeres, they say that could translate into an average gain of about 4.5 years of life.

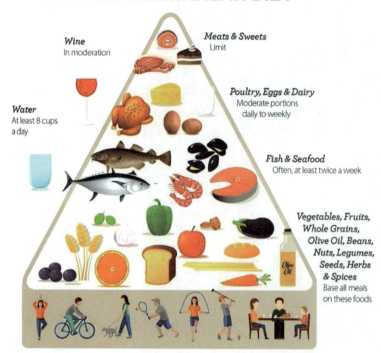

It's good for the heart, it's good for the brain, it's good for the waistline, if diet can modify how we age on a cellular level, that's a big deal.

The diet rich in fish, nuts, vegetable's, olive oil, even red wine is also associated with a decreased risk of heart disease and cancer.

This is the first time a study actually showed that women ___5___ not only looked better, felt better, but internally their cells appear younger.

For good morning America, Reena N, ABC news, New York.

(　　) A. who followed a Mediterranean diet

(　　) B. the Mediterranean diet keeps them intact

(　　) C. Mediterranean diet may extend your life

(　　) D. who adhere to a Mediterranean diet

(　　) E. the popular Mediterranean diet can be good for your body

Unit 3 | Intangible Cultural Heritage and Regional Development

Task 3 Role-play in pairs according to the situation given below. The expressions given below are for your reference.

In an interview, Interviewer A is asking Candidate B about his/her favorite music/sport/book/movie/dish…

- Are you a music lover?
- … is the most important thing in my life.
- What kinds of music do you like best?
- I like… music very much. I spend one hour or two everyday listening to them.
- Really? I like… music too.
- Are you fond of… songs?
- Of course. I like them. I think they are nice.
- No. I think it is noisy.
- Who's your favorite singer?
- Why do you like him/her?

Task 4 Listen to the passage and choose the best answer.

1. How does the speaker feel about American people and states?
   A. Bored.   B. Amazed.
   C. Amused. D. Indifferent.

2. What do Americans have in common according to the speaker?
   A. The way they treat holidays.
   B. The food they have during holidays.
   C. The love they have to their hometowns.
   D. The way they cherish memories.

3. What makes Thanksgiving so particular?
   A. It is the longest holiday for all Americans.
   B. It is the most interrupted holiday.
   C. It is the most purely American of holidays.
   D. It is the ideal holiday to travel.

4. When did the Pilgrims settle down in the country?
   A. 300 years ago.   B. 350 years ago.
   C. 400 years ago.   D. 450 years ago.

5. Why is Thanksgiving so special to the speaker?
   A. Because he can have delicious food on that day.
   B. Because it brings him beautiful memories in life.
   C. Because it means the reunion of the whole family.
   D. Because he can run away from work for a few days.

Task 5 Listen to the passage and fill in the blanks.

A few months ago, I was down with a terrible cold which ended in a persistent bad cough. No matter how many ___1___ remedies I tried, I still couldn't get rid of the cough. Not only did it inconvenience my teaching but also my life as a whole. Then one day after class, a student came up to me and ___2___ ___3___ Chinese medicine. From her description, Chinese medicine sounded as if it had magic power that worked ___4___. I was hesitant because I knew so little about it and have never tried it before. Eventually, my cough got so much ___5___ that I couldn't sleep at night, so I decided to give it a try. The Chinese doctor took my pulse and asked to see my tongue, both of which were new ___6___ to me because they are both non-existent in Western medicine. Then the doctor gave me a scraping (刮) treatment known as "Guasha". I was a little ___7___ at first because he used a smooth edged tool to scrape the skin on my neck and shoulders. A few minutes later, the pressured strokes started to ___8___ a relieving ___9___ and my body and mind began to sink deeper into relaxation. I didn't feel any improvement in my ___10___ in the first couple of days, but after a few more regular visits to the doctor, my cough started to lessen. Then within a matter of weeks, it was completely gone!

Task 6 Role-play in pairs according to the situation below. The expressions given below are for your reference.

In an interview, Interviewer A is asking Candidate B about his/her family/hometown/country/local specialty/festival…

- Please say something about your family.
- Do you usually help your parents with the housework?
- Could you introduce some interesting place in your hometown?
- Can you tell me the most famous local food/snacks in your hometown?
- How do you feel about being away from home frequently?
- I come from…, one of the most beautiful cities in China.
- In my hometown, you can enjoy wonderful scenery and delicious seafood.
- I was born and grew up in southern China. Welcome to my hometown!
- What's your nationality?
- What's your favorite festival? Say something about it.

Pre-reading questions

1. How is the pandemic impacting living heritage?
2. In what way has the living heritage helped communities recover from the pandemic?

Living heritage and the COVID-19 pandemic: responding, recovering and building back for a better future

Living heritage during the pandemic

The impact of the pandemic has been far-reaching and devastating. It has also highlighted the importance of our interconnectedness and common humanity. For many communities struggling with or recovering from the pandemic, living heritage has become an important source of resilience, helping to overcome social and psychological challenges and strengthen ties. In the past year, communities have adapted how they practice their living heritage to unexpected situations, highlighting the resilience of living heritage and our reliance on it.

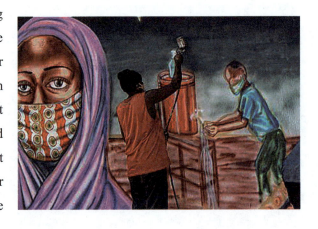

There can, of course, be no living heritage without the people who practice and transmit it. At the same time, the restrictions put in place to counter the spread of the COVID-19 virus have reminded us that we cannot thrive without the practices that we inherited from our ancestors and which define us. The pandemic has highlighted the value of intangible cultural heritage and the importance communities attach to its continued practice and expression.

In April 2020 the Living Heritage Entity launched an online survey aimed at grasping the impact of the COVID-19 pandemic around the world. Thanks to the active participation of numerous cultural actors, UNESCO received more than 200 testimonies from 78 countries. The "Living Heritage in the face of the COVID-19 pandemic" report, now available online, summarizes the results of the survey and the challenges and opportunities for living heritage during this crisis. It looks at three key questions and provides answers to the following:

1. How is the pandemic impacting living heritage?
2. How is living heritage adapting to the crisis?
3. How are communities mobilizing their living heritage to help them face the pandemic?

Recommendations for post recovery plans

Although many countries are still in the midst of the pandemic, debates are already sparking worldwide on what the future will look like and what we can do to build back better for future generations. To contribute to these discussions, survey participants were asked to share their opinion on what could be done from the lens of living heritage to recover from the COVID-19 pandemic. Their inputs were summarized in three key recommendations detailed in the report, providing essential insight about how to integrate living heritage into post-pandemic recovery plans.

Recommendation 1: Help communities build back better by strengthening recovery support mechanisms to living heritage bearers at the local level, including through local governance structures.

Recommendation 2: Take advantage of digital technologies to increase the visibility and understanding of living heritage.

Recommendation 3: Strengthen and amplify the linkages between safeguarding living heritage and emergency preparedness, response and recovery plans and programs.

(429 words)

New words

▲impact	/ˈɪmpækt/	n.	巨大影响
pandemic	/pænˈdemɪk/	n.	流行病
*far-reaching	/ˌfɑːˈriːtʃɪŋ/	a.	深远的
devastating	/ˈdevəsteɪtɪŋ/	a.	毁灭性的
interconnectedness	/ˌɪntəkəˈnektɪdnəs/	n.	关联性
resilience	/rɪˈzɪliəns/	n.	恢复力；弹力；适应力
▲psychological	/ˌsaɪkəˈlɒdʒɪkl/	a.	心理的
▲unexpected	/ˌʌnɪkˈspektɪd/	a.	出乎意料的；始料不及的
*reliance	/rɪˈlaɪəns/	n.	依赖
▲transmit	/trænzˈmɪt/	v.	传输
▲restriction	/rɪˈstrɪkʃn/	n.	限制
▲counter	/ˈkaʊntə(r)/	v.	抵制；抵消
thrive	/θraɪv/	v.	兴旺发达；繁荣
testimony	/ˈtestɪməni/	n.	证据；证明
▲summarize	/ˈsʌməraɪz/	v.	总结；概括；概述
▲crisis	/ˈkraɪsɪs/	n.	危机
▲mobilize	/ˈməʊbəlaɪz/	v.	调动；调用
▲spark	/spɑːk/	v.	引发；触发
▲insight	/ˈɪnsaɪt/	n.	洞察力

mechanism	/ˈmekənɪzəm/	n.	方法；机制
visibility	/ˌvɪzəˈbɪləti/	n.	可见度
amplify	/ˈæmplɪfaɪ/	v.	放大，增强
▲safeguard	/ˈseɪfɡɑːd/	v.	保护；保障；捍卫
▲emergency	/ɪˈmɜːdʒənsi/	n.	突发事件；紧急情况
*preparedness	/prɪˈpeərɪdnəs/	n.	（尤指对战争或灾难）有准备，做好准备

Phrases & expressions

highlight the importance of	强调……的重要性
common humanity	共同的人道主义精神，共同的人性
struggle with	与……作斗争
recover from	从……恢复
adapt… to…	使……适应……
put in place	就位，启用
attach importance to	重视
thanks to	幸亏；归因于
in the midst of	在……当中
contribute to	有助于；促成
integrate… into…	与……成为一体
take advantage of	利用

Proper names

the Living Heritage Entity	活态文化遗产实体
living heritage bearers	活态文化遗产传承人
COVID-19	新型冠状病毒肺炎（Corona Virus Disease 2019）

生词数	生词率	*B级词汇	*A级词汇	▲四、六级词汇	超纲词汇
25	5.8%	1	2	13	9

Notes

1. **For many communities struggling with or recovering from the pandemic, living heritage has become an important source of resilience, helping to overcome social and psychological challenges and strengthen ties.**

   对于许多正在与这一流行病作斗争或正在恢复的社区来说，活态文化遗产已成为恢复力的重要来源，有助于克服社会和心理挑战并加强联系。

   struggling with or recovering from…为现在分词短语做后置定语，修饰其前面的名词communities；helping to…为现在分词短语做伴随状语，修饰句子中由谓语表示的主要动作。

2. **There can, of course, be no living heritage without the people who practice and transmit it.**

当然，没有实践和传播遗产的人，就不会有活态文化遗产。

本句为否定词no/not/never等 + without构成的双重否定句式。双重否定句形式上虽为否定，实则表示强烈的肯定语气，如No smoke without fire（无风不起浪）。

3. **Although many countries are still in the midst of the pandemic, debates are already sparking worldwide on what the future will look like and what we can do to build back better for future generations.**

尽管许多国家仍处于这场流行病之中，但全世界已经在就未来会是什么样子及我们可以做些什么来为子孙后代更好地重建家园展开辩论。

宾语从句what the future will look like…做介词on的宾语。

4. **Their inputs were summarized in three key recommendations detailed in the report, providing essential insight about how to integrate living heritage into post-pandemic recovery plans.**

他们的建议总结在报告中详述的三项关键建议中，为如何将活态文化遗产纳入后疫情恢复计划提供了重要见解。

were summarized为一般过去时的被动语态，providing为现在分词短语做伴随状语。

After-reading tasks

Task 1 Answer the following questions according to Reading B and then discuss them with your classmates.

1. How is living heritage adapting to the crisis?

2. What have the restrictions against the COVID-19 virus reminded us?

3. Why did the Living Heritage Entity launch an online survey in April 2020?

4. What do the three key recommendations provide?

5. How will living heritage help communities build back better?

Task 2 Translate the following sentences into Chinese.

1. In the past year, communities have adapted how they practice their living heritage to unexpected situations, highlighting the resilience of living heritage and our reliance on it.

2. We cannot thrive without the practices that we inherited from our ancestors and which define us.

3. To contribute to these discussions, survey participants were asked to share their opinion on what could be done from the lens of living heritage to recover from the COVID-19 pandemic.

4. Take advantage of digital technologies to increase the visibility and understanding of living heritage.

5. Strengthen and amplify the linkages between safeguarding living heritage and emergency preparedness, response and recovery plans and programs.

Comprehensive exercises

Task 1 Fill in the blanks with the words or phrases from Reading A and Reading B that match the meanings in the column on the right. The first letter of each word is given.

1. i_____ the powerful effect that sth. has on sb./sth.
2. v_____ several different, diverse
3. s_____ to become stronger; to make sb./sth. stronger
4. i_____ abstract or hard to define or measure
5. h_____ to emphasize sth., especially so that people give it more attention
6. d_____ the food that you eat and drink regularly
7. f_____ likely to have a lot of influence or many effects
8. p_____ to keep sb./sth. alive, or safe from harm or danger
9. i_____ _____ in answer to
10. i_____ _____ to combine two or more things so that they work together

Task 2 Fill in the blanks with the words given below in proper forms.

| cuisine | grant | unique | maintain | thrive |
| remind | pandemic | numerous | celebration | thanks to |

1. They held a party in _____ of their victory.
2. The digital publishing industry is _____ nowadays.
3. He was proud of his son's remarkable and _____ performance.
4. You must _____ him to take his medicine, in case he forgets.
5. The advantages of this system are too _____ to mention.
6. The hotel offers not only western food but also typical Chinese _____.
7. Wherever and whenever a _____ starts, everyone around the world is at risk.
8. The bank finally _____ me a 500-pound loan.
9. _____ recent research, effective treatments are available.
10. We shall _____ our focus on the needs of the customer.

Task 3 Rewrite the following sentences after the models.

Model 1: There can, of course, be no living heritage if there aren't people who practice and transmit it.
→There can, of course, be *no* living heritage *without* the people who practice and transmit it.

1. We cannot succeed if you don't help.

_____

2. If you don't respond by tomorrow, we cannot continue the project.

_____

Model 2: The intangible cultural heritage tries to preserve living heritage by merely guarding the processes. Oral history collects all the historical detail and then preserve them.
→The intangible cultural heritage tries to preserve living heritage by merely guarding the processes *while* oral history collects all the historical detail and then preserve them.

1. Some people waste food. Others haven't enough.

_____

2. Mary likes to turn the large rooms into traditional French style. Howard prefers a typical English look.

_____

Task 4 — Translate the following sentences into English, using the given phrases.

1. 有时候，在客户服务方面，小公司可以胜过大公司。(when it comes to)

2. 他们高度重视这个项目。(attach importance to)

3. 本书是根据个人经历写成的。(be based on)

4. 他们常借用民歌来传递历史。(pass down)

5. 文化多元化是当今世界的鲜明特征。(diversity)

Applied writing

Invitation letter (邀请信)

邀请信是写信人对收信人的盛情邀约，一般分为正式和非正式两种。就本质而言正式与非正式的邀请信并没有什么区别，只是正式的邀请信比较注意文采，而且往往需要表现出更大的热忱。邀请信的格式与其他信函的相同，具体写作步骤如下：

首段：说明与收信人的相关性和邀请信的写作意图。

主体段落：具体交代背景，包括受邀请的人、邀请对方做什么、地点及具体的时间等内容，并且强调为什么邀请收信人而不是其他人。

结尾段：表示期待被邀请人的回复。

Sample 1 Formal invitation

Tues. June 20, 2021

Dear Ms. Liu,

  On behalf of Dean Gordon Lee and Kwantlen College, I am extending to you our formal invitation to visit Kwantlen campus.

  We have arranged meeting between you and Mr. Lee at 10:00 A.M. on June 21. We would like to make you the guest of the College for an overnight stay at the College Club on June 21. We are all expecting you to visit our campus.

Sincerely Yours,
Alice Wong
Manager
International Programs

Sample 2 Informal invitation

Aug. 15th, 2021

Mr. Anderson,

    I was very glad to learn from your letter that you will be in Beijing next week and I'd be delighted if you could spare an hour for lunch on August 30 at the Holiday Inn.

    Unless I hear further from you, I'll plan to meet you in the foyer of the Holiday Inn at about twelve thirty.

Ted Li

Writing task

Write a letter of invitation according to the following instructions given in Chinese.

请你以中兴学院学生会主席刘明的名义给李老师写一封邀请信，邀请他7月10日晚上7点30分在T-103教室，参加"探寻非物质文化遗产传承人"主题抖音短视频启动会，并让李老师作简短讲话，鼓励学生们暑假期间深入家乡实景拍摄非遗传承人，领略中华文化之美。

Words for reference

学生会：the Students Union
主席：chairperson
传承人：inheritor
抖音短视频：Tiktok vlog
启动会：launching ceremony

Unit 3 | Intangible Cultural Heritage and Regional Development

Project performing

Event organizing

When organizing an event, you must think of the marketing mix—the 5Ps:

- people—performers/audience/participants/entertainment
- product—type of event: Decide what event is going to be. Decide who will organize the event and be responsible for its successful outcome.
- price—tickets/entry/sponsor: Budgets should cover everything, all income and expenditure.
- place—where: Decide on the best venue. The location is vital: is it easy to reach? Does it have sufficient car parking? Is it easy to access by public transport?
- period—date/day/time: Picking the date and time of an event can make it or break it. When will most people be able to attend? Is there a weather factor to take into account?

 Exercises

Suppose the 7th China ICH Expo, the country's largest ICH event, will open on Sept 13 in your province, offering a platform to display the country's rich and colorful cultural legacies as well as its achievements in intangible cultural heritage protection. Branch activities of the expo will be held in your school to help the younger generation learn more about China's rich traditional culture and improve their artistic accomplishments. Now try to organize an ICH event. Discuss the following clues in your group, adding necessary details. Please make a presentation in the class.

Organizing an ICH event (非遗学堂进校园)

People
非遗传承人、30名学生

Product: interactive exhibition
剪纸传承人现场教授、学生体验中国剪纸魅力

Price
政府出资，学生免费体验

Place
T-110教室

Period
9月17日周五下午

Grammar

Predicative clause (表语从句)

在句中作表语的从句叫表语从句。引导表语从句的关联词与引导主语从句的关联词大致一样，表语从句位于系动词之后。其基本结构可分为两类："be + that"型从句和"be + 疑问词"型从句。

1. "be + that"型从句

The fact is that we have lost the game.
事实是我们已经输掉了这场比赛。

The reality is that the party must be cancelled because of the storm.
现实就是因为暴风雨这个聚会必须得取消了。

2. "be + 疑问词"型从句

The question is whether they will help us.
问题是他们会不会帮我们。

The problem is why she didn't go back home directly.
问题是为什么她没直接回家。

That's what I want. 这正是我想要的。

This is where our problem lies.
这就是我们的问题所在。

It looks as if it is going to rain. 看起来天要下雨了。

注意：

1. 表语从句使用陈述语序

The question is when he can arrive at the hotel. 问题是他什么时候能到酒店。

2. 当主句主语是reason时，表语从句要用that引导，不可用because

The reason why he was late was that he missed the train by one minute this morning.
他迟到的原因是今天早上他误了一分钟火车。

Task 1 — Underline and correct the mistake in each of the sentences, paying attention to the predicative clause.

1. The problem is we are short of money.
2. Things are not that they seemed to be.
3. Our city is no longer it used to be.
4. The question is how we can do about it.
5. The reason why we were late was because we missed the bus.
6. The question is if the movie is worth seeing.

Task 2 — Choose the best answer to complete the sentences.

1. —I drove to Zhuhai for the air show last week.
   —Is that _____ you had a few days off ?
   A. why B. what C. when D. where

2. I had neither a raincoat nor an umbrella. _____ I got wet through.
   A. It's the reason B. That's why C. There's why D. It's how

3. See the flags on top of the building? That was _____ we did this morning.
   A. when B. which C. where D. what

4. —Are you still thinking about yesterday's game?
   —Oh, that's _____.
   A. what makes me feel excited
   B. whatever I feel excited about
   C. how I feel about it
   D. when I feel excited

5. What surprised me was not what he said but _____ he said it.
   A. the way B. in the way that C. in the way D. the way which

Self-evaluation

Rate your own progress in this unit.	D	M	P	F*
I can tell others what ICH is.	☐	☐	☐	☐
I can say different types of ICH in English.	☐	☐	☐	☐
I can name some inventories of ICH in China and in my hometown.	☐	☐	☐	☐
I can tell others the new situation of Living Heritage during COVID-19.	☐	☐	☐	☐
I can write letters of invitation in English.	☐	☐	☐	☐
I have mastered Predicative Clauses.	☐	☐	☐	☐

*Note: D (Distinction), M (Merit), P (Pass), F (Fail)

Culture

The following is a news item from *China Daily*, in which Liuzhou luosifen is listed as intangible cultural heritage in China. Listen to the news item and finish the tasks.

Task 1 Listen to the news item and then read the script.

A total of 185 new cultural practices and expressions, including the preparation of luosifen, have been inscribed on the latest list of national intangible cultural heritage released by the State Council.

The latest fifth list brings the total number of national intangible cultural heritage practices to 1,557, according to the State Council figures.

Liuzhou luosifen, a soup dish dubbed by some people as the "durian of soup" for its strong smell, originated in Liuzhou, a city in South China's Guangxi Zhuang autonomous region.

It features rice vermicelli soaked in a spicy broth flavored by river snails and topped with ingredients including pickled bamboo shoots, string beans, peanuts and tofu skin.

Despite having the word "snail" in its Chinese name, actual snails don't commonly appear in the dish, but are used to flavor the broth.

Xinhua reports that the annual sales of river snail rice noodles in more than 20 countries and regions exceeded 10 billion *yuan* ($1.54 billion) in 2020, while providing over 250,000 jobs across the industrial chain.

Task 2 Discuss the following questions in groups.

1. Please find out the words describing luosifen in the video, and then describe the flavor of river snail rice noodles in your own words.
2. Please discuss the success story of luosifen in terms of intangible cultural heritage and industrial chain.
3. What's the specialty of your hometown? Is there any intangible cultural heritage in your hometown? What would you do to make it a big industry?

Unit 4
The Rise of Guochao

Learning objectives

After studying this unit, you should be able to:
- enlarge vocabulary related to Guochao;
- get to know the rise of Guochao in China.
- write letters of complaint in English;
- master how to use the appositive clause.

Warm-up

Task 1 The following pictures are some Chinese brand logos. Match each picture to the accurate names in English.

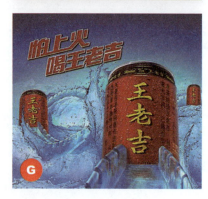

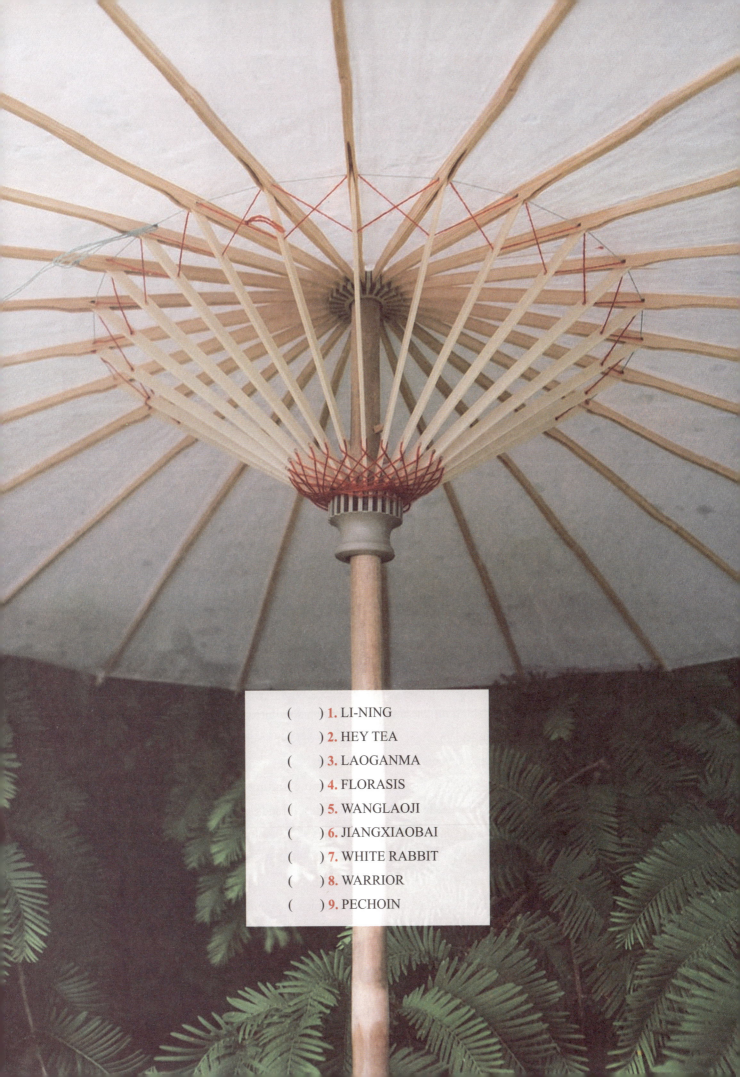

(　) 1. LI-NING
(　) 2. HEY TEA
(　) 3. LAOGANMA
(　) 4. FLORASIS
(　) 5. WANGLAOJI
(　) 6. JIANGXIAOBAI
(　) 7. WHITE RABBIT
(　) 8. WARRIOR
(　) 9. PECHOIN

Task 2 Watch the video and complete the following tasks.

1. Watch the video and then read the script.

A new trend is taking hold in China. The related keyword was searched for over 12.6 billion times in 2018, and from January to July 2019 that number increased by nearly 400%.

What made Chinese customers so hyped up? "China Chic".

This term refers to fashion trends native to China. Its initial connotation was similar to that of "Brit Style", which incorporates unique native cultural elements into latest trends.

After "China Chic" witnessed its massive success in the clothing industry, its impact continued to extend to various industries. The cosmetic and food industries have brought back traditional visual motives such as cranes and flower-and-bird paintings by incorporating them into packaging designs. The film, television and music industries have also given new life to traditional cultural heritages, through mediums such as classical literature and the musical instrument, Guzheng, enabling them to make a grand comeback into the lives of the younger generation.

To this day, "China Chic" means much more than an innovative Chinese style that demonstrates one's unique fashion sense; it also includes the retro Chinese styles that represent traditional parts of Chinese culture.

There are multiple factors that led to the revival of "China Chic". On the one hand, there is the collective innovation of Chinese brands in taking on the country's traditional culture. On the other hand, the mentality shift of Chinese customers has also had an effect. When it comes to fashion and trends, pop culture from Japan, Korea and the West has long influenced young Chinese customers.

However, now with "China Chic" rising on the scene, more and more Chinese youth are becoming interested in buying products that are made in China, by Chinese brands. According to China's Consumer Trend Index 2019 by Nielsen, 68% of Chinese consumers prefer Chinese brands. Among them, 62% indicated that they are open to international brands. However, local brands are still regarded as their priority choice.

Today, Chinese brands are able to offer the world much more than just "made in China". More significantly, they are exporting China's culture and aesthetic, which are bound to make a lasting difference.

2. Discuss the following questions in groups.

(1) According to the video, why did "China Chic" make Chinese customers so hyped up?

(2) Please discuss the cultural elements embodied in some Chinese and international brands that you are familiar with.

Reading A

Pre-reading questions

1. Have you ever heard of Guochao?
2. What's your understanding of Guochao?

Guochao

Over the past few years, China has seen a surge in young consumers' interest in domestic brands and products that incorporate Chinese traditional style and culture, a trend known as Guochao.

The story of Guochao began in 2011 when Feiyue and Huili, both Chinese sneaker brands, suddenly gained international attention. Their products were seen on models all over the world. Chinese sportswear brand Li-Ning was at the New York Fashion Week in September with new designs—hoodies and jackets decorated with Chinese characters.

China's young adults, particularly those between the ages of 20—25, grew up in a different environment than previous generations. They have seen the rise of China as a global economic powerhouse. China's young people are now more confident about their own culture. Western culture doesn't have the instant appeal to the young that it once had. Today's young people in China are passionate about Chinese cultural elements. They like these elements printed on their clothes, even the brand image of laoganma—the famous chili sauce in China—which was once seen as outside of fashion. But now young people are proud of these Chinese symbols.

As this age demographic is becoming one of China's largest spending groups, domestic brands have quickly jumped at this opportunity—more established and previously considered outdated brands such as Li-Ning and Pechoin are rebranding themselves to appeal to younger audiences, brands popular in the early 2000s such as White Rabbit and Wanglaoji are drawing on nostalgia, and new brands such as Perfect Diary, Hey Tea, and Zhongxuegao are appearing out of nowhere and achieving incredible sales with their guerilla marketing strategies.

Guochao is not only about the rise of domestic brands, but also the resurgence of traditional style and cultural elements. Beijing's historical Forbidden City has become extremely popular among Chinese youths due to its numerous product design collaborations with both domestic and international brands and influencers.

(338 words)

New words

*surge	/sɜːdʒ/	n.	激增
*generation	/ˌdʒenəˈreɪʃən/	n.	世，代，辈
▲powerhouse	/ˈpaʊəhaʊs/	n.	强国
*appeal	/əˈpiːl/	n.	吸引力，魅力
*passionate	/ˈpæʃənət/	a.	热情的，狂热的
▲demographic	/ˌdeməˈɡræfɪk/	n.	（尤指特定年龄段的）人群
*rebranding	/ˌriːˈbrændɪŋ/	n.	重塑形象
nostalgia	/nɒˈstældʒə/	n.	怀旧；恋旧
guerilla	/ɡəˈrɪlə/	n.	游击队
▲resurgence	/rɪˈsɜːdʒəns/	n.	复苏

Phrases & expressions

known as	被称为
be confident about	对……有信心
appeal to	对……有吸引力
outside of fashion	与时尚无关
out of nowhere	突然出现
be achieving with	用……达到
be popular among	受……欢迎
due to	由于

Proper names

New York Fashion Week	纽约时装周
Guerilla marketing	游击营销
the Forbidden City	故宫

生词数	生词率	*B级词汇	*A级词汇	▲四、六级词汇	超纲词汇
10	3%	4	1	3	2

Notes

1. **Over the past few years, China has seen a surge in young consumers' interest in domestic brands and products that incorporate Chinese traditional style and culture, a trend known as Guochao.**
   在过去的几年里，中国的年轻消费者对融入中国传统风格和文化的国内品牌和产品的兴趣激增，这一趋势被称为国潮。

that引导的定语从句修饰前面的domestic brands and products。

2. **The story of Guochao began in 2011 when Feiyue and Huili, both Chinese sneaker brands, suddenly gained international attention.**

"国潮"的故事始于2011年，中国运动鞋品牌飞跃和回力突然引起了国际社会的关注。

when引导的定语从句，修饰2011年。

After-reading tasks

Task 1 Decide whether each of the following statement is true or false according to Reading A.

(　　) 1. Today's young Chinese have inherited the way of life of previous generations.
(　　) 2. Western culture does not immediately appeal to Chinese young people as it once did.
(　　) 3. White Rabbit and Wanglaoji are opening many stores by using guerilla strategies.
(　　) 4. The Forbidden City has developed many cultural and creative products with many cultural elements, which are highly sought after by young people.

Task 2 Complete the mind map below with the understanding of Reading A.

Guochao culture

What is Guochao?	Guochao is a phenomenon, it needs to have two elements: First, it must have the genes of Chinese ___1___ and ___2___; second, it must be integrated with the current trend and have a more fashionable ___3___.
The rise of Guochao	The rise of the Guochao is due to the rapid ___4___ of national power and ___5___, which brings cultural self-confidence and cultural return.
The different types of brand strategies	Li-Ning and Pechoin are redesign their brand ___6___ to ___7___ young consumers. White Rabbit and Wanglaoji are building brand's ___8___. Perfect Diary's strategy is ___9___ marketing strategy.

Listening and speaking

Task 1 Listen to the dialogue and answer the following questions.

1. What was Henry doing on Friday night when his problems started?
   A. He was watching a game on TV with some friends.
   B. He was seeing his wife off at the airport.
   C. He was having a barbeque with some friends.
   D. He was playing a game with some friends.
2. How was the vase broken?
   A. Henry's friends kicked it because they were very excited.
   B. Henry accidentally dropped it.
   C. One of Henry's friends bumped into it with his arm.
   D. One of Henry's friends was too excited to hold the vase. It burned up in a fire.
3. How did the manuscript of the book become totally ruined?
   A. It burned up in a fire.
   B. Hot water damaged the entire copy.
   C. Someone mistakenly threw it into the trash.
   D. It was soaked in blue ink.
4. How will his wife feel when she got the whole story?
   A. Disappointed.   B. Furious.
   C. Satisfied.   D. Unhelpful.

 Task 2 Listen to the news report and number the sentences in the order you have heard.

The topic of my talk today is gift-giving. Everybody likes to receive gifts, right? So you may think that gift-giving is a universal custom. But actually, ____1____, and not knowing them can result in great embarrassment. In North America, the rules are fairly simple. If you're invited to someone's home for dinner, ____2____. Among friends,

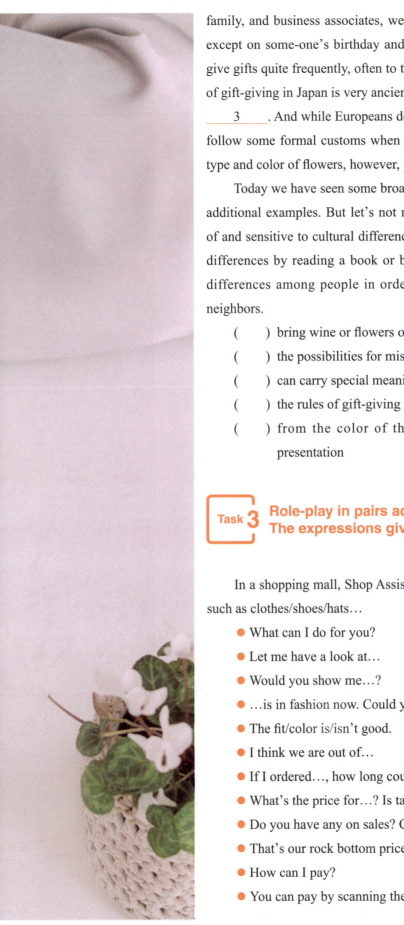

family, and business associates, we generally don't give gifts on other occasions except on some-one's birthday and Christmas. The Japanese, on the other hand, give gifts quite frequently, often to thank someone for their kindness. The tradition of gift-giving in Japan is very ancient. There are many detailed rules for everything ____3____. And while Europeans don't generally exchange business gifts, they do follow some formal customs when visiting homes, such as bringing flowers. The type and color of flowers, however, ____4____.

Today we have seen some broad differences in gift-giving. I could go on with additional examples. But let's not miss the main point here: If we are not aware of and sensitive to cultural differences, ____5____. Whether we learn about these differences by reading a book or by living abroad, our goal must be to respect differences among people in order to get along successfully with our global neighbors.

(   ) bring wine or flowers or a small item from your country
(   ) the possibilities for miscommunication and conflict are enormous
(   ) can carry special meaning
(   ) the rules of gift-giving vary quite a lot
(   ) from the color of the wrapping paper to the time of the gift presentation

Task 3 Role-play in pairs according to the situation given below. The expressions given below are for your reference.

In a shopping mall, Shop Assistant A is recommending goods to Customer B, such as clothes/shoes/hats…

- What can I do for you?
- Let me have a look at…
- Would you show me…?
- …is in fashion now. Could you try…?
- The fit/color is/isn't good.
- I think we are out of…
- If I ordered…, how long could it take before I got delivery?
- What's the price for…? Is tax already included in this price?
- Do you have any on sales? Can you make it cheaper?
- That's our rock bottom price. There is a promotion going on for …% off.
- How can I pay?
- You can pay by scanning the QR code.

Task 4 Listen to the passage and choose the best answer.

1. What did the speaker most probably discuss last time?
   A. Creativity as shown in arts.
   B. A major scientific discovery.
   C. Famous creative individuals.
   D. The mysteriousness of creativity.

2. What is a widely accepted idea about the creative process?
   A. It is the source of all artistic work.
   B. It starts soon after we are born.
   C. It is something people all engage in.
   D. It helps people acquire knowledge.

3. What leads to major scientific discoveries according to the speaker?
   A. Natural curiosity.
   B. Critical thinking.
   C. Logical reasoning.
   D. Creative imagination.

4. What does the speaker imply about the creative process?
   A. It is part of everyday life.
   B. It is a unique human trait.
   C. It is yet to be fully understood.
   D. It is beyond ordinary people.

Task 5 Listen to the passage and fill in the blanks.

The nationwide EU-China Training Project for Clerical Staff ____1____ started in Beijing following the launch of a piloting program in Wuhan, Hubei Province.

The ____2____ is designed to improve the ____3____ of Sino-EU joint ventures. Any enterprise in any ____4____ will be able to discuss training requests with foreign ____5____ and jointly ____6____ training programs. Helped by European and Chinese experts the project will not only train clerical staff, but also ____7____ the Chinese education system by employing the latest European training ____8____. Most of the project's services will be ____9____.

The piloting program in Wuhan, ____10____ with 15 million euros from the EU Commission and Hubei Province, will improve staff in Sino-EU joint ventures over the next five years. Another 40 projects will go in other provinces and in different companies.

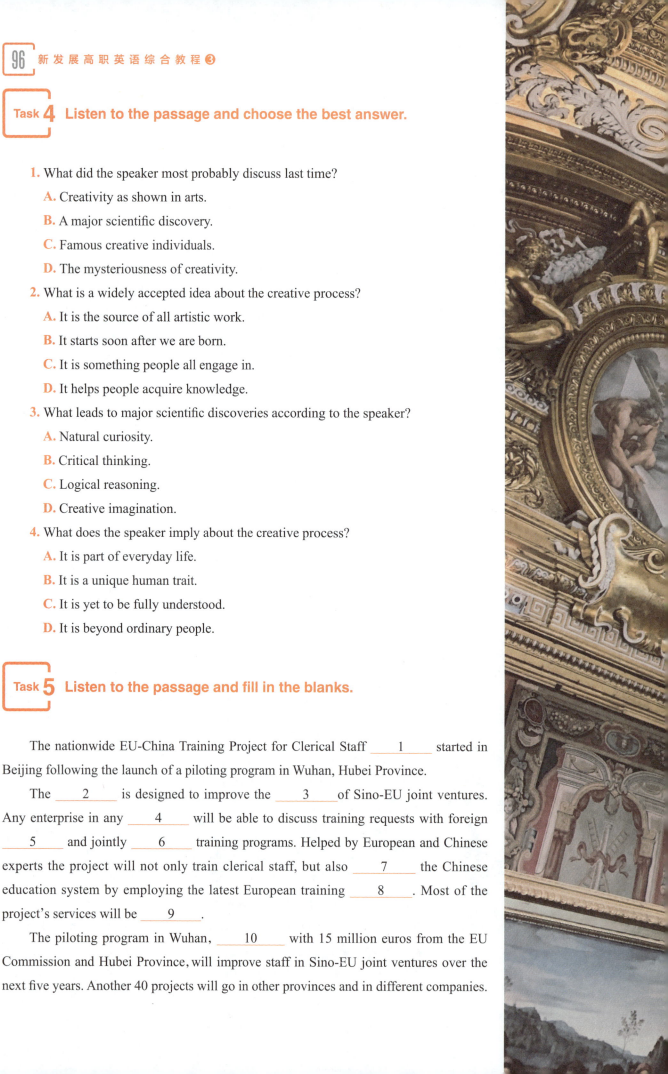

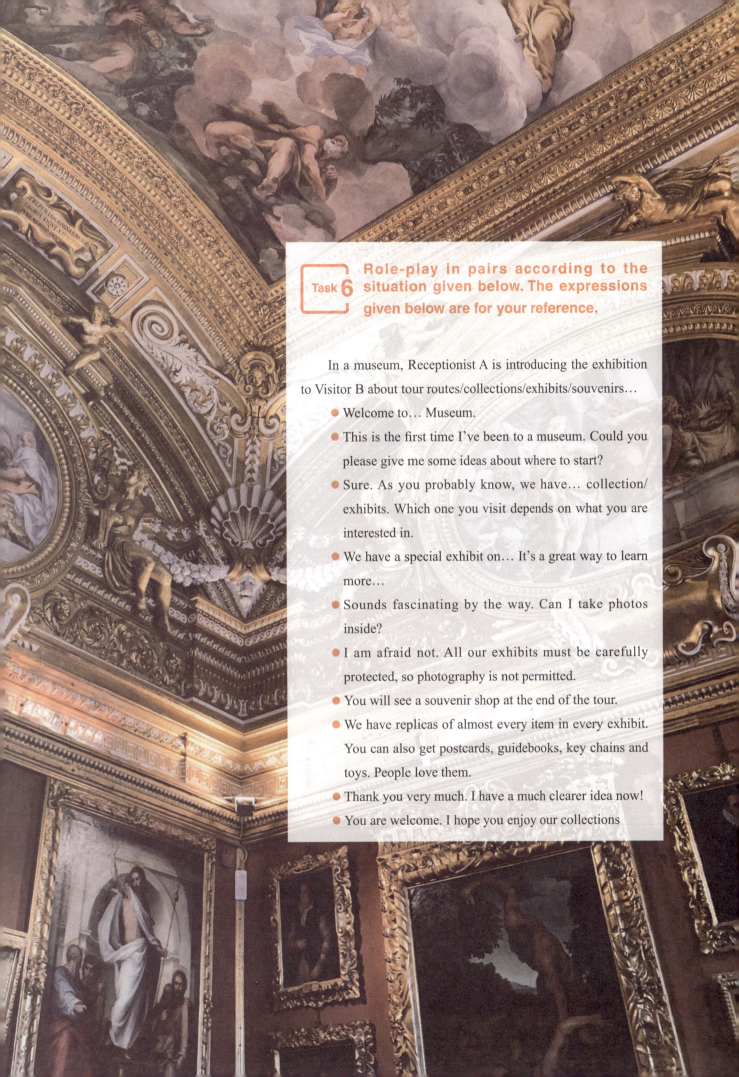

Task 6
Role-play in pairs according to the situation given below. The expressions given below are for your reference.

In a museum, Receptionist A is introducing the exhibition to Visitor B about tour routes/collections/exhibits/souvenirs…

- Welcome to… Museum.
- This is the first time I've been to a museum. Could you please give me some ideas about where to start?
- Sure. As you probably know, we have… collection/exhibits. Which one you visit depends on what you are interested in.
- We have a special exhibit on… It's a great way to learn more…
- Sounds fascinating by the way. Can I take photos inside?
- I am afraid not. All our exhibits must be carefully protected, so photography is not permitted.
- You will see a souvenir shop at the end of the tour.
- We have replicas of almost every item in every exhibit. You can also get postcards, guidebooks, key chains and toys. People love them.
- Thank you very much. I have a much clearer idea now!
- You are welcome. I hope you enjoy our collections

Reading B

> **Pre-reading questions**
> 1. Why did the tide of the state rise?
> 2. Do you know any story of Chinese brands?

The rise of national brand originates from the unprecedented patriotic style

In the traditional impression of many people, "domestic" are always inferior to "foreign products" in high-end atmosphere, which is particularly prominent in the clothing industry. Take sportswear brands as an example. An ordinary T-shirt can be sold for more than 200 by foreign brand Nike, but Anta, a domestic brand, can only sell 80%—90%. Should domestic brands always be inferior to others?

In 2018, domestic sportswear brand Li-Ning appeared in New York autumn and winter fashion week with its "Wudao" and "China lining" series. With its unique Chinese cultural elements and original design concept, "Wudao" soon became "powder" after it was released. Many young people in China have expressed that "the original tomato fried eggs can still be so popular?"

Li Ning, who once had no relationship with fashion, opened the door of the new fashion of the national trend by relying on the "Enlightenment" with Chinese style. At this point, the national tide officially rose.

Why did the tide of the state rise?

On the one hand, with the state's attention to national culture, traditional culture embarked on the road of rejuvenation. From the popularity of Chinese Poetry Conference to the popularity of Nezha: Birth of the Demon Child, more and more young people feel the breadth and profundity of Chinese culture. In addition, under the influence of Sino-US trade disputes and other events, Chinese people's sense of national identity and pride has been growing, and patriotism has become a cool thing. The Chinese cultural elements and cultural connotations displayed by Guochao show a unique sense of fashion under the performance of modern fashion forms. Young people who pursue personality display are naturally willing to embrace and even praise Guochao products.

On the other hand, with the rapid development of China's economy and society, the basic material needs such as food and clothing are no longer the focus of Chinese people's attention. People are more eager to meet the spiritual and cultural level, which is fully reflected in the consumption concept of young people. The consumer groups in Z era not only care about the practicability of products, but also care about whether the products can meet their own personalized needs, and show their unique trend attributes, so as to obtain more sense of belonging and identity.

In the current era of national fashion, in order to recapture the Chinese market occupied by overseas fashion brands, how should China's clothing brands make efforts?

In order to become a real fashion brand, on the one hand, it is necessary to select the appropriate elements of Guochao to make them fit with the attributes of the products. Because the fashion brand clothing does not mechanically copy all kinds of fashionable cultural elements to the clothes, but the products themselves contain a certain kind of popular culture. The integration of the same attribute trend elements makes this culture continuously radiate new vitality.

On the other hand, through bold and innovative original design, domestic sports brand Li-Ning has realized the combination of Chinese elements and fashion clothing, which has brought different visual experience to the public, and thus opened the door of new fashion of Guochao.

At last, do a good job in marketing, improve the brand's popularity and activity, tell the story behind the national fashion + clothing, let consumers start from appearance, and finally culture. Of course, the promotion of the brand cannot be completed overnight, but as long as Guochao clothing brands persist for a long time, it is believed that it will eventually become the "supreme" in China.

(589 words)

New words

▲inferior	/ɪnˈfɪərɪə/	a.	差的, 低等的
▲atmosphere	/ˈætməsfɪə(r)/	n.	气氛; 氛围
▲prominent	/ˈprɒmɪnənt/	a.	突出的, 显著的
enlightenment	/ɪnˈlaɪtənmənt/	n.	启蒙
▲embark	/ɪmˈbɑːk/	v.	登上
rejuvenation	/rɪˌdʒuːvəˈneɪʃən/	n.	复兴
profundity	/prəˈfʌndɪtɪ/	n.	深度
▲dispute	/ˈdɪspjuːt/	n.	纠纷, 争端
▲patriotism	/ˈpeɪtrɪətɪzəm/	n.	爱国主义
connotation	/ˌkɒnəˈteɪʃən/	n.	内涵
*practicability	/ˌpræktɪkəˈbɪlɪtɪ/	n.	实用性, 可行性
▲attribute	/ˈætrɪˌbjuːt/	n.	特征, 特性, 属性
*mechanically	/mɪˈkænɪklɪ/	ad.	使用机械地; 机动地; 在机械方面; 机械上; 机械地
integration	/ˌɪntɪˈgreɪʃən/	n.	结合; 集成; 一体化; 整合
▲radiate	/ˈreɪdɪˌeɪt/	v.	辐射; 发散; 从中心发散; 呈辐射状发出
*vitality	/vaɪˈtælətɪ/	n.	活力; 生机; 生命力; 生存力
▲ideological	/aɪdɪəˈlɒdʒɪkl/	a.	思想观念上的; 思想体系的; 意识形态的

Phrases & expressions

be inferior to	不如
under the influence of	在……的影响下
be eager to	渴望
so as to	以便
as long as	只要

Proper names

Chinese Poetry Conference	中国诗词大会
Nezha	哪吒（中国古代神话传说中的神仙，佛教及道教护法神）
Z era	Z世代（美国及欧洲的流行用语，意指在1995—2009年间出生的人，又称网络世代、互联网世代，统指受到互联网、即时通信、短讯、MP3、智能手机和平板电脑等科技产物影响很大的一代人）

生词数	生词率	*B级词汇	*A级词汇	▲四、六级词汇	超纲词汇
17	2.8%	1	2	9	5

Notes

1. **Many young people in China have expressed that "the original tomato fried eggs can still be so popular?"**
   国内不少年轻人纷纷表示"原来番茄炒鸡蛋还能这么火？"
   tomato fried eggs意为"番茄炒蛋"。李宁服装红色和黄色的色彩搭配在国人的印象中一直都是"土味"代表。不过在纽约时装周上，它也着实让大家惊艳了一把，可以把"番茄炒蛋色"设计得那么时髦。

2. **Young people who pursue personality display are naturally willing to embrace and even praise Guochao products.**
   追求个性彰显的年轻人自然愿意拥抱甚至赞美国潮产品。
   定语从句who pursue personality display做主语young people的修饰语。

3. **People are more eager to meet the spiritual and cultural level, which is fully reflected in the consumption concept of young people.**
   人们更渴望精神文化层面的满足，这充分体现在年轻人的消费观念上。
   be more eager to更加渴望……。which引导非限制性定语从句，指代句子People are more eager to meet the spiritual and cultural level。

4. **Of course, the promotion of the brand cannot be completed overnight, but as long as Guochao clothing brands persist for a long time, it is believed that it will eventually become the "supreme" in China.**

当然，该品牌的推广不能在一夜之间完成，但只要国家服装品牌持续很长时间，人们相信它最终将成为中国的"至尊"。

as long as 意为"只要"。it is believed that 是一般现在时的被动语态，为固定句型，其中 it 是形式主语，that 后面的句子才是真正的主语。

After-reading tasks

Task 1 Answer the following question according to Reading B.

What should Chinese clothing brands do to break the dilemma of fashion brands?

Task 2 Translate the following sentences into Chinese.

1. Li Ning, who once had no relationship with fashion, opened the door of the new fashion of the national trend by relying on the "Enlightenment" with Chinese style.

2. In addition, under the influence of Sino-US trade disputes and other events, Chinese people's sense of national identity and pride has been growing, and patriotism has become a cool thing.

3. The consumer groups in Z era not only care about the practicability of products, but also care about whether the products can meet their own personalized needs, and show their unique trend attributes, so as to obtain more sense of belonging and identity.

Comprehensive exercises

Task 1 Fill in the blanks with the words or phrases from Reading A and Reading B that match the meanings in the column on the right. The first letter of each word is given.

1. i_____   a new thing or a new method of doing something
2. r_____   to take again
3. a_____   to be attractive, interesting
4. p_____   love for your country and loyalty towards it
5. n_____   an affectionate feeling you have for the past, especially for a particularly happy time
6. o_____   a foreign country or foreign countries collectively
7. a_____   suitable or acceptable for a particular situation
8. p_____   depth
9. s_____ _____ _____   in order to
10. p_____ _____   to continue steadfastly or firmly in some state, purpose, course of action, or the like

Task 2 Fill in the blanks with the words given below in proper forms.

| foundation | illiterate | unprecedented | pursue | conscience |
| decorations | view | individual | revolutionary | perspiration |

1. Whether you are old or young, educated or _____, you can appreciate it as long as you can see.
2. A good _____ is a soft pillow.
3. Genius is one percent inspiration and ninety-nine percent _____.
4. In the rural areas of northern China windows are often covered with paper-cuts as window _____.
5. When an _____ enters a strange culture, he or she is like fish out of water.
6. If they throw stones at you, don't throw back, use them to build your own _____ instead.
7. Accept what was and what is, and you'll have more positive energy to _____ what will be.
8. Having grown up in Beijing, I am familiar with the Chinese _____ stories.
9. China's economic success has accentuated its new development concepts _____ in human history.
10. The current contemporary international system was structured according to a Western world _____.

Unit 4 | The Rise of Guochao

Task 3 Rewrite the following sentences after the models.

Model 1: Mother went to bed after she finished the housework.

→Mother did *not* go to bed *until* she finished the housework.

1. The scientist had supper after he finished his work at midnight.
   _____
   _____.

2. I realized how important it was to study hard after I failed in the college entrance examination.
   _____
   _____.

Model 2: The rain has stopped. Let's go for a walk.

→Since the rain has stopped, let's go for a walk.

1. We are young. We shouldn't be too afraid of making mistakes.
   _____
   _____.

2. Lily has obviously forgotten to phone me. I'll have to telephone her.
   _____
   _____.

Task 4 Translate the following sentences into English, using the given phrases.

1. 我们需要吸引更广泛的客户。(appeal to)
2. 一些著名香水品牌，不仅在当时被称为整个欧洲销量最大的香水，而且至今仍在全球最受欢迎香水中名列前茅。(be popular among)
3. 如果孩子感觉自己不如其他孩子，他的信心就会减弱。(inferior to)
4. 这种设计后来被称为东方风格。(known as)
5. 只要为人正直，别人就会尊敬你。(as long as)

Applied writing

Letters of complaint (投诉信)

投诉信是某人对所提供的服务或所购买的商品不满意时，向商家、机构提出相关的问题，并希望问题得到解决和处理所写的信件。这类信件的写作要点通常包括以下几部分：

1. 提出写信的目的是抱怨或投诉
2. 表明投诉的原因
3. 希望问题能够得到解决

Sample 1 Complaint concerning service

Dear Sir or Madam,

　　I was a visitor in your hotel for three days during May 5 to May 8. I am sorry I have to say I was greatly disappointed with the inconvenient service you provided.

　　First of all, it is the lighting facility in the room. One of the lights is broken and another is so dark. Another unpleasant factor of your hotel is the food quality. The steak I ordered is sour. The last but not the least shortcoming of your hotel is the cold and indifferent service of the waiters. I asked one of them to bring newspaper to my room, but no paper was delivered at last.

　　I am sure that you will agree with me that your service is unacceptable. I trust that you will take immediate steps to correct the situation and I look forward to your reply.

Faithfully yours,
John Smith

Sample 2 Complaint concerning damaged goods

Dear Mr. Smith,

The 50 Tea Sets we ordered were delivered yesterday, but we regret that 5 sets were badly damaged.

The packages containing the tea sets appeared to be in good condition, so we accepted and signed for them without question. We unpacked the tea sets with great care and can only assume that the damage must be due to careless handling at some stage prior to packing.

We shall be glad if you will replace all the 50 sets as soon as possible. Meanwhile, we have put the damaged tea sets aside in case you need to check them.

Yours sincerely,
David

Writing task

Write a letter of complaint according to the following instructions given in Chinese.

你上周在一家商店买了一部数码相机，你发现它出了问题。写信给商店经理解释这个问题，并表达你的抱怨和建议解决方案。

Words for reference

冒昧，斗胆：venture   替换，更换：exchange   方案：solution

Project performing

Feedback processing

When dealing with feedback, you should follow the five stages of feedback processing:

Feedback processing flow

Stage 1	Add to customer complaint log	Record detailed customer feedback, including feeders, time, content, demands, etc.
Stage 2	Investigate nature of feedback	After understanding the content of customer feedback, determine the nature of customer feedback and whether the appeal is reasonable. If the appeal is unreasonable, you can refuse the customer in a gentle way to obtain the customer's understanding.
Stage 3	Propose and implement treatment suggestions	According to the content of feedback and the nature of the problem, find the responsible person to follow up the case and put forward appropriate solutions.
Stage 4	Provide information on results to customer	Feed back the results of processing to the feeders.
Stage 5	Update customer feedback log	Summarize and comprehensively evaluate the processing process, and update the customer feedback log.

Suppose you are the manager of the public relations department of a hotel and receive an email from a customer named Zhang Fei who gives feedback on the accommodation experience.

The content of the email is: the hotel environment is very good, the service is good, the room is clean and tidy, the food is delicious, and the overall experience is very good. However, the hotel is far from the city center. It is recommended that the hotel add a shuttle bus from the hotel to the subway station, so as to provide convenience for guests.

Please discuss how to deal with this feedback in groups, and then make a presentation in the class.

Please finish the project step by step.

Exercises

1. Group discussion

(1) Work in small groups of 3 to 4 students;

(2) Talk about the main point of this case;

(3) Share your ideas within the group.

2. Presentation

(1) Volunteers give presentations to the whole class;

(2) Introduce how to deal with this case. Make sure to include five stages of feedback processing.

3. Communication and composition

(1) Discuss with your teacher and classmates about difficulties;

(2) After discussion, write down your plans of feedback processing.

Grammar

Appositive clause (同位语从句)

同位语从句指的是在复合句中充当同位语的从句，属于名词性从句的范畴，用来对其前面的抽象名词进行解释说明。同位语从句一般用that, whether, what, which, who, when, where, why, how等词引导，常放在fact, news, idea, truth, hope, problem, information, wish, promise, answer, evidence, report, explanation, suggestion, conclusion等抽象名词后面，说明该名词的具体内容。换言之，同位语从句和所修饰的名词在内容上为同一关系，对其内容作进一步说明。

1. 由that引导的同位语从句

若同位语从句意义完整，应用that引导同位语从句（that不充当任何成分，只起连接作用，不可省略）。

The general gave the order that the soldiers should cross the river at once.

将军下达了战士们立即过河的命令。

析：the soldiers should cross the river at once是the order的全部内容，且意义完整。因此应用that引导同位语从句。

2. 由whether引导的同位语从句

若同位语从句意义不完整，需增加"是否"的含义，应用whether引导同位语从句（if不能引导同位语从句）。

We'll discuss the problem whether the sports meeting will be held on time.

我们将讨论运动会是否会如期举行的问题。

析：the sports meeting will be held on time意义不完整，应加"是否"的含义才能表达the problem的全部内容。因此应用whether引导同位语从句。

3. 由连接代词引导的同位语从句

若同位语从句意义不完整，需增加"谁""什么""谁的""哪个"等含义，应用who, whom, whose, which等词引导同位语从句。

I am wondering the puzzle who has taken away my umbrella.

我想知道是谁拿走了我的雨伞。

4. 由连接副词引导的同位语从句

若同位语从句意义不完整，需增加"什么时候""什么地点""什么方式"等含义，应用when, where, how等词引导同位语从句。

I have no idea when he will be back.

我不知道他什么时候会回来。

析：he will be back意义不完整，应加"什么时候"的含义才能表达idea的全部内容。因此应用when引导同位语从句。

5. 当主句的谓语较短，而同位语从句较长时，同位语从句常后置。

The thought came to him that maybe the enemy had fled the city.

他突然想到，也许敌人已经逃离了这座城市。

The story goes that she has won the race many times.

据说她已经赢得了很多次比赛。

Task 1 Underline and correct the mistake in each of the sentences, paying attention to the appositive clause.

1. John has no idea that his mom went away without any words.

2. We'll never forget the days that we studied in college.

3. Our city is no longer it used to be.

4. The question is how we can do about it.

5. The reason why we were late was because we missed the bus.

6. The question is if the movie is worth seeing.

Task 2 Choose the best answer to complete the sentences.

1. The fact _____ she works hard is well known to us all.
   A. why   B. that   C. when   D. which

2. Have you any idea _____ time it starts?
   A. if   B. how   C. what   D. when

3. We are not investigating the question _____ he is trustworthy.
   A. why   B. which   C. where   D. whether

4. We haven't yet settled the question _____ we are going to spend our summer vacation.
   A. where   B. when   C. how   D. if

5. The rumour spread _____ a new school would be built here.
   A. /   B. that   C. when   D. which

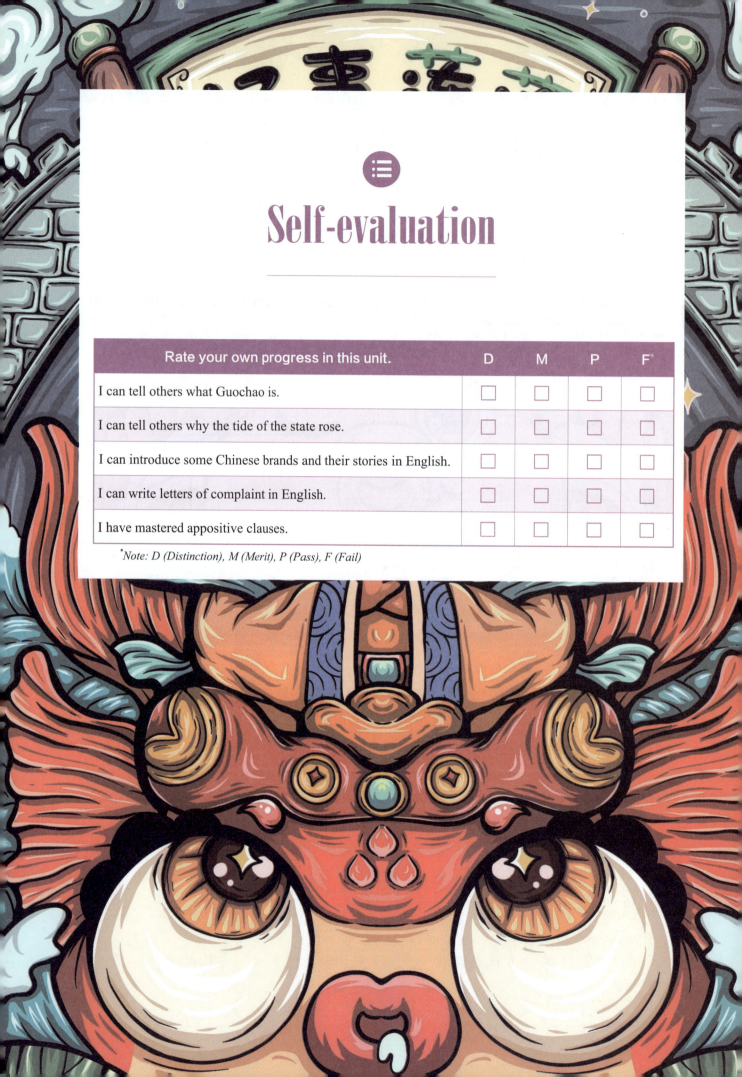

Self-evaluation

Rate your own progress in this unit.	D	M	P	F*
I can tell others what Guochao is.	☐	☐	☐	☐
I can tell others why the tide of the state rose.	☐	☐	☐	☐
I can introduce some Chinese brands and their stories in English.	☐	☐	☐	☐
I can write letters of complaint in English.	☐	☐	☐	☐
I have mastered appositive clauses.	☐	☐	☐	☐

*Note: D (Distinction), M (Merit), P (Pass), F (Fail)

Culture

Cultural confidence is a more basic, deeper and more lasting force in the development of a country and a nation. Only a self-confident civilization can absorb and draw on the achievements of other civilizations while maintaining its own characteristics. The Chinese nation will not be able to rejuvenate itself without strong cultural confidence and a rich and prosperous culture.

Watch the video clip and try to get the main idea of the speech.

My grandpa is a fevered fan of Chinese calligraphy. I can still remember those loving afternoons in his study several years ago. Sitting on his lap. I'd stretch out my puppy-fat tiny hands, following his brush to imitate every word as peaceful characters emerged on the paper one after another. But one day his hands suddenly became paralyzed in mid-air.

He had had a stroke, and that meant he could no longer do calligraphy. However, instead of being sorrowful, he gave me a broadest, purest, and proudest smile I had ever seen, saying, "How lucky I am that they are all in my blood." I was too young to exactly understand what he meant, but later on when I reflected on that oversized grin. I was just amazed by how deeply Chinese culture was engraved in his mind and how naturally this cultural confidence had registered from a normal Chinese individual's words and actions. Those words of my grandpa, "They're all in my blood", will ring true to every Chinese person. The first word we spoke, Chinese; the first thing we wrote, a Chinese character; and the first bedtime story my mommy ever told me, a Chinese legend. All these seemingly common issues will strike a chord with every Chinese person, and channeling new inspiration to us today. On May 22 this year, China's Zhurong rover landed on Mars and has operated for more than two months and traveled more than 300 meters. Intriguingly, it's named Zhurong the god of fire in Chinese mythology, which adds a sense of romance into this ice-cold machine, and strikes a chord with all of Chinese. With traditional culture channeling new inspiration, the problem is anything but how to be culturally confident, but instead how we cannot be. However, simply being confident is just a start, a preparation for a further excursion and a prelude for a greater episode. When we dig deeply with thorough insight into our own culture, we will find many things still need to be perfected and some things in pressing need of a revival. And my friends, this mission lies on us Chinese youth. In 1962 a 24-year-old Peking university graduate set foot in the Gobi Desert where a unique cultural hub, Mogao Grottoes, needed urgent protection. The graduate said, "I was there because I was needed there." Though doing countless things for these significant relics, Fan Jinshi said the only thing she was doing was staying there. Every time I turn the pages of her biography her tiny figure walking step by step on the vast desert will reemerge in my mind. Though we may work in different fields, fight for different dreams, the quality we need is the same: staying power. I always dream of being an intercultural communicator. Cause every time I am left dizzy when I find a connection between ancient and modern, oriental and occidental culture, and there is a strong impulse inside me to share this pleasure with everyone else. But I know the road of pursuit is definitely full of barriers and obstacles. To conquer this, what we need is a strong cultural confidence and a firm stay on our way. After the stroke, my grandpa shifted his focus towards studying ancient characters, and he has developed a habit of smelling ink. As he said, that sweet scent of ink is conducive to his recovery. And my friends, facing the new and embracing the old, let's march confidently to the new era with a sweet scent of ink lingering in our mind! Thank you very much!

Task 1 Answer the following question.

What is the dream of the girl who gives the speech?

Task 2 Discuss the following topic in groups.

Talk about any aspect of Chinese culture which is "in your blood". Share your ideas with your classmates.

Unit 5
Work Ethics and Job Security

Learning objectives

After studying this unit, you should be able to:
- get familiar with the words and expressions concerning work ethics and job security;
- understand the meaning and importance of work ethics;
- understand the status quo of China's employment market;
- talk about emerging professions and industries;
- write a request for leave;
- master how to use conditional sentences.

Warm-up

Task 1 Watch the video of an interview and write down the key words in each person's description. The words given below are for your reference.

> hardworking   dependable   cohesive   competitive

Team-oriented. I believe that you can go further as a group and working as a _____ team.

_____.

Slightly _____, as well as being a _____ and give _____.

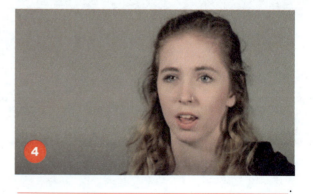

_____.
You got to do _____, no matter what.

Task 2 Talk about your ideas based on the video.

Why is work ethic important?

Reading A

> **Pre-reading questions**
>
> 1. What's your understanding of work ethic?
> 2. How should one improve one's work ethic?

A strong work ethic

Employers want to work with people who have a strong work ethic. Those who possess this trait are better employees who get the job done, no matter what. They often require less oversight on daily activities and managers are able to rely on them to complete bigger tasks. Here are five factors to look for that demonstrate a strong work ethic.

Always behaves professionally

Professionalism is something observed from the moment an employee walks in the office door to when he leaves. He is professionally dressed with clean, pressed clothes. He arrives a few minutes early to settle in and get his coffee, so that he will be ready to start his shift on time. He is courteous to other employees and doesn't take random breaks or change lunch schedules without authorization. He understands his job and is prepared to do it. Work ethics set the tone to develop the habits needed to be professional and consistent all day long.

Organization and high productivity

Employees with strong work ethics tend to follow or develop daily tasks. These are often ordered and organized so that he knows he is able to devote the required time to any task. For example, the first two hours might be to respond to customer calls and new orders. Then, the next two hours might be devoted to sales calls. He could then use the afternoon to prepare new proposals and do administrative work that is required, so his desk is cleared before he leaves for the night. Having a routine and being organized increases productivity. Employees with this trait simply get more done.

Teamwork and cooperation

Part of having a strong work ethic is understanding that you are part of a bigger team and that everyone has a role. This understanding fosters teamwork and cooperation to ensure that everyone is getting the right information to properly do their jobs. And since those with strong work ethics tend to be more productive and efficient with their time, it frees up time to help others to get more done. The person with a strong work ethic isn't looking at what he needs to get done; he is looking at what needs to get done for the company to succeed. He is a team player.

Determined to succeed

Those with a strong work ethic have an internal motivation to succeed, which can be seen in everything they do. It could be a simple computer issue that is causing frustration. An employee with a strong work ethic won't wait for someone else to deal with the problem. He will call the right resources, search online for remedies and work the problem until it is resolved. This determination to success permeates everything he does.

Consistent and high-quality work

Because of proper scheduling, a determination to succeed and a high standard of professionalism, the work produced by an employee with a strong work ethic is good. Not only is work presented in a neat and professional manner, but it often goes above and beyond what was required initially.

For example, you might ask an employee to fold the new inventory of sweaters. Someone with a strong work ethic not only folds them but organizes them by size or color and asks what is needed next. He will clean the area where they are to be displayed so everything is orderly and neat for customers to view.

(565 words)

New words

▲ethic	/ˈeθɪk/	n.	道德；伦理；行为准则
*possess	/pəˈzes/	v.	拥有，具有
▲trait	/treɪt/	n.	特征，特性，品质
▲require	/rɪˈkwaɪə(r)/	v.	需要；要求
▲oversight	/ˈəʊvəsaɪt/	n.	监督；监察；监管
▲manager	/ˈmænɪdʒə(r)/	n.	经理；主管
*complete	/kəmˈpliːt/	v.	完成；完工；使完整
*factor	/ˈfæktə(r)/	n.	因素；要素
▲demonstrate	/ˈdemənstreɪt/	v.	显示；表明
▲behave	/bɪˈheɪv/	v.	行事，表现
▲shift	/ʃɪft/	n.	班；轮班
*courteous	/ˈkɜːtiəs/	a.	有礼貌的；谦恭有礼的
*random	/ˈrændəm/	a.	任意的；随机的；胡乱的
▲authorization	/ˌɔːθəraɪˈzeɪʃn/	n.	批准，准许；授权
▲consistent	/kənˈsɪstənt/	a.	一贯的；坚持的；始终如一的

▲devote	/dɪˈvəʊt/	v.	将……贡献给，把……奉献给
▲proposal	/prəˈpəʊzl/	n.	建议；计划；提案
▲administrative	/ədˈmɪnɪstrətɪv/	a.	管理的；行政的
▲productivity	/ˌprɒdʌkˈtɪvəti/	n.	生产力；生产率；生产能力
▲foster	/ˈfɒstə(r)/	v.	促进；鼓励
▲ensure	/ɪnˈʃʊə(r)/	v.	确保；保证
▲internal	/ɪnˈtɜːnl/	a.	内部的，内在的
▲motivation	/ˌməʊtɪˈveɪʃn/	n.	积极性，干劲；动机，诱因
*issue	/ˈɪʃuː/	n.	问题；议题
▲frustration	/frʌˈstreɪʃn/	n.	挫折；沮丧
▲remedy	/ˈremədi/	n.	补救办法；疗法
▲determination	/dɪˌtɜːmɪˈneɪʃn/	n.	决心；毅力
▲permeate	/ˈpɜːmieɪt/	v.	渗透；弥漫；遍布；充满
▲manner	/ˈmænə(r)/	n.	方式，方法
*beyond	/bɪˈjɒnd/	prep.	更远；远于
initially	/ɪˈnɪʃəli/	ad.	最初，一开始
▲fold	/fəʊld/	v.	折叠，对折
▲display	/dɪˈspleɪ/	v.	陈列；展示
▲orderly	/ˈɔːdəli/	a.	整齐的；有序的

💬 Phrases & expressions

rely on	依靠，依赖
settle in	迁入，安顿
take breaks	休息
set the tone	奠定基调
free up	解放
be determined to do sth.	下定决心做某事
deal with	处理
call the resources	整合资源
search online for...	在线搜索……
organize... by...	依据……组织……

生词数	生词率	*B级词汇	*A级词汇	▲四、六级词汇	超纲词汇
34	6%	5	2	26	1

After-reading tasks

Task 1 Tick off the qualities that are considered to demonstrate a strong work ethic according to Reading A.

☐ 1. professionally dressed
☐ 2. be courteous to others
☐ 3. be ordered and organized
☐ 4. always arrive a few minutes earlier
☐ 5. wait for others to solve the problem
☐ 6. always get himself a cup of coffee
☐ 7. go beyond the initial requirement
☐ 8. be determined to succeed

Task 2 Read the passage again and decide whether each of the following statement is true (T) or false (F). If it is false, write the key words to support your answer.

( ) 1. An employee with a strong work ethic behaves professionally throughout the whole day of work.

( ) 2. A courteous employee doesn't take breaks randomly or change lunch schedules without permission.

( ) 3. Having a routine and being organized increase leadership.

( ) 4. A person with a strong work ethic understands that he is part of a bigger team and that everyone has a role to play.

( ) 5. The work produced by an employee with a strong work ethic is usually presented in a neat and professional manner, and is even better than the original requirement.

Listening and speaking

Task 1 Listen to the dialogue three times and choose the best answer.

1. A dress code refers to the standards of what is _____ to wear to work.
   A. pretty   B. proper   C. clean   D. expensive

2. Dress codes vary from place to place based on _____.
   A. the need of the workplace   B. the interests of the employees
   C. the cost of the clothing   D. the weather and climate

3. Casual dress is what you would probably NOT wear _____.
   A. at Tech firms   B. at grocery stores   C. to meet clients   D. to watch sporting events

4. _____ are NOT required to wear a uniform to work.
   A. Police officers B. Factory workers C. Salespeople   D. Waiters

5. Li Ming _____ workplace dress codes before this conversation.
   A. knows a lot about   B. knows something about   C. knows little about   D. does not care about

Task 2 Listen to the passage three times and discuss the following questions with your classmates.

1. Do you think it is necessary to wear high heels or not?
2. How can we improve women's experience in the workplace?

△ Nicola Thorp, who was sent home from work over refusal to wear high heels, criticises decision not to change legislation outside the Commons.

Task 3 Listen to the dialogue three times and fill in the blanks.

Li Ming: Good morning, Mr. Wang.

Mr. Wang: Good morning, Li Ming.

Li Ming: Mr. Wang, I'm going to start my first intern next week. But I'm still not sure how to work ____1____. Could you help me?

Mr. Wang: Sure, my pleasure. In order to work efficiently and productively, you need to have good ____2____. You need to plan your time wisely.

Li Ming: How can I do this?

Mr. Wang: Here are some useful tips for you. It is important for you to make a to-do list before starting a whole day's work. Firstly, you need to ____3____ to be done and ____4____ them. To prioritize means to put the tasks in order of ____5____, so that you can deal with the important ones first. Next, try to set ____6____ to each task on your list, instead of just working until they're done. This helps you ____7____, so you won't end up a day without ticking off anything.

Li Ming: Good idea! I will try to follow your advices.

Mr. Wang: And of course, don't forget to ____8____ in between. You can take short breaks between each task and a longer break after completing four or five. Keeping ____9____ between work and rest help ____10____ and maintain motivation.

Li Ming: Sounds great! Thank you so much, Mr. Wang.

Mr. Wang: You're welcome.

Unit 5 | Work Ethics and Job Security 121

Task 4 Liu Mei, a student, designed the following table to help organize a whole day's work. Discuss the following questions with your classmates.

	Urgent	Not urgent
Important	**Do** · Finish the first draft · Finish the powerpoint	**Decide** · Book the room for weekly team meeting · Check the mailbox
Not important	**Delegate** · Organize team activity · Answer customer calls	**Delete** · Attend the online meeting · Review the conference proceedings

△ Liu Mei's to-do table

1. How does Liu Mei organize the tasks?
2. Which one would you do first, the important task or the urgent task? Why?
3. How do you like this table?

Task 5 Make up a dialogue and give your partner some advice on improving the efficiency and quality of work. Some sentences are given for your reference.

- Avoid doing several tasks at the same time.
- Group similar tasks together.
- Eliminate distractions, such as social media, web browsing, chatting with co-workers, and instant messaging.
- Learn to say no if you can't finish everything.

Reading B

Flexibility in China's employment market

China's urban unemployment rate recovered to pre-pandemic levels in March 2021 to 5.3 percent, after reaching a record high of 6.2 percent in February 2020, when JD Logistics announced that the company had created over 20,000 new jobs to help with deliveries.

The increase in China's unemployment rate from 2019 to 2020 was lower than that of the United States, the European Union and Russia. China's growing gig economy helped to cushion unemployment during the pandemic, reflecting the strengthening flexibility among the country's workers.

How has this flexibility trend developed in the employment market over the past decades? Firstly, urban employees had limited career choices in earlier times. In the 1950s, the government allocated urban residents to work in the dominant state-owned enterprise sector. By the 2000s, "flexible employment" was being promoted, and more people chose to work outside of the state sector, whether as self-employed persons or in private businesses. As a result, urban employees at state sector declined by about 41 percent from 1992 to 2008, while those in the private sector increased more than nine-fold.

When it came to the 2010s, the time of "Internet Plus", job seekers with appropriate skills started to utilize online platforms and to take up emerging professions, such as home organizer and mobile app designer. The internet makes it possible for people to work without the limits of time and space, leading to the acceleration of the gig economy. The flexible employee market in China experienced a compound annual growth rate of 45 percent between 2016 and 2019—from about 155 billion *yuan* ($24 billion) to about 478 billion *yuan* ($74 billion), according to a recent report.

Secondly, the mobility of the employee market for non-agricultural workers in rural areas has also increased. In the 1950s, rural residents were advised not to blindly migrate to cities for jobs. These restrictions were later eased. As urbanization and the services sector took the lead among the three economic sectors, increasing numbers of job seekers in rural areas started to migrate to cities. Not only are they flowing to the more developed eastern areas, but they are also finding more opportunities in the western region.

Thirdly, a young generation with entrepreneurial spirit and growing pursuit of autonomy launched businesses of their own. They became more actively engaged in high-

tech and internet industries and even took the lead globally. According to a CB Insights report, in 2019, China had 107 unicorn start-ups—young private companies with a valuation of over $1 billion—ranking second around the world behind America's 214. China has nine of the 32 "super unicorns", which have a valuation of more than $10 billion.

At the same time, higher labor market flexibility has its own risks. There are increasing concerns about the insurance and benefits of migrant workers from rural areas. Society is expecting more laws and regulations to protect the interests of this vulnerable group.

(486 words)

📖 New words

▲urban	/ˈɜːbən/	a.	城市的，城镇的
*announce	/əˈnaʊns/	v.	（尤指公开地）宣布，宣告，通告
*create	/kriˈeɪt/	v.	创造；创建；创作；发明
▲delivery	/dɪˈlɪvəri/	n.	运送，递送，投递
*cushion	/ˈkʊʃn/	v.	对（某事物的影响或力量）起缓冲作用
*reflect	/rɪˈflekt/	v.	反射（光、热、声等）；反映，映出（影像）
*strengthen	/ˈstreŋθn/	v.	增强，加强；巩固
*limited	/ˈlɪmɪtɪd/	a.	有限的；不多的，少量的
allocate	/ˈæləkeɪt/	v.	分配；分派；拨给，划拨
*resident	/ˈrezɪdənt/	n.	居民，住户
▲dominant	/ˈdɒmɪnənt/	a.	主要的；主导的；占优势的
*promote	/prəˈməʊt/	v.	促进；促销，推销；推广
*percent	/pəˈsent/	n.	百分之……（符号为%）
*appropriate	/əˈprəʊpriət/	a.	适当的，恰当的；合适的
*utilize	/ˈjuːtəlaɪz/	v.	使用；利用；应用
acceleration	/əkˌseləˈreɪʃn/	n.	增速，加快；加速性能
mobility	/məʊˈbɪləti/	n.	活动性；流动性
*rural	/ˈrʊərəl/	a.	乡村的，农村的；似乡村的
▲migrate	/maɪˈɡreɪt/	v.	（指人）大批外出；（暂时）移居，迁移
▲urbanization	/ˌɜːbənaɪˈzeɪʃn/	n.	城市化；城市化过程
*flow	/fləʊ/	v.	流动
*opportunity	/ˌɒpəˈtjuːnəti/	n.	机遇，时机，机会；可能性
▲pursuit	/pəˈsjuːt/	n.	追求；从事；实行
autonomy	/ɔːˈtɒnəmi/	n.	自治，自治权；自主
*launch	/lɔːntʃ/	v.	启动，推出，发起
*engage	/ɪnˈɡeɪdʒ/	v.	雇用；聘用
globally	/ˈɡləʊbəli/	ad.	全球地；全局地；世界上
*risk	/rɪsk/	n.	风险；危险

*insurance	/ɪnˈʃʊərəns/	n.	保险
*benefit	/ˈbenɪfɪt/	n.	利益，好处；优势
*regulation	/ˌreɡjuˈleɪʃn/	n.	规则，条例，法规；控制，管理
*interest	/ˈɪntrəst/	n.	利益，好处
▲vulnerable	/ˈvʌlnərəbl/	a.	易受伤的；易受影响的；脆弱的

Phrases & expressions

take up	开始从事；开始学习；拿起
make it possible (for...) to...	使（某人）做某事成为可能
lead to	导致
launch a business	创业
take the lead	带头，领先

Proper names

JD Logistics	京东物流
gig economy	零工经济
Internet Plus	互联网+
CB Insights	智库（全球知名的市场数据研究平台）

生词数	生词率	*B级词汇	*A级词汇	▲四、六级词汇	超纲词汇
33	6.8%	12	9	7	5

Notes

1. Gig economy

"零工经济"指由工作量不多的自由职业者构成的新经济领域，利用互联网和移动技术快速匹配供需方，主要包括群体工作和经应用程序接洽的按需工作两种形式。"零工经济"是共享经济的一种重要的组成形式，是人力资源的一种新型分配形式。

2. Internet Plus

"互联网+"即"互联网+传统行业"，指依托互联网信息技术实现互联网与传统产业的联合，以优化生产要素、更新业务体系、重构商业模式等途径来完成经济转型和升级。

3. Compound annual growth rate

年复合增长率是一项投资在特定时期内的年度增长率，英文常缩写为CAGR。

4. Not only are they flowing to the more developed eastern areas, but they are also finding more opportunities in the western region.

他们不仅涌入较为发达的东部地区，同时也在西部地区寻找更多机会。该句采用"not only..., but also..."句式，表示"不仅……还……"；"not only"置于句首时须用倒装句。

5. Unicorn

"独角兽企业"指估值在10亿美元以上的初创企业,由风险投资家Aileen Lee于2013年提出。截至2020年,全世界约有600家独角兽企业。

After-reading tasks

Task 1 Complete the table below with the understanding of Reading B.

Group of People	Major Change	Supporting Details
Urban employees	Having more ___1___	In the 1950s, urban residents worked in the dominant ___2___.
		By the ___3___, more people chose to work as ___4___ or in ___5___.
		In the 2010s, the time of "___6___", job seekers utilized ___7___ and took up ___8___.
Non-agricultural workers in ___9___ areas	Increasing in ___10___	In the ___11___, rural residents were advised not to ___12___.
		Later, ___13___ were eased and rural job seekers started to move to cities.
The young generation	Launching business of their own	Young people were more actively engaged in ___14___ industries and even took the lead globally.

Task 2 Translate the following paragraph into Chinese.

When it came to the 2010s, the time of "Internet Plus", job seekers with appropriate skills started to utilize online platforms and to take up emerging professions, such as home organizer and mobile app designer. The internet makes it possible for people to work without the limits of time and space, leading to the acceleration of the gig economy. The flexible employee market in China experienced a compound annual growth rate of 45 percent between 2016 and 2019—from about 155 billion *yuan* ($24 billion) to about 478 billion *yuan* ($74 billion), according to a recent report.

Comprehensive exercises

Task 1 Fill in the blanks with the words or expressions from Reading A and Reading B that match the meanings in the column on the right. The first letters are given.

1. c_____ polite and showing respect
2. p_____ to have or own sth., or to have a particular quality
3. a_____ suitable or right for a particular situation or occasion
4. d_____ the ability to continue trying to do sth., although it is very difficult
5. p_____ to encourage people to like, buy, use, do, or support sth.
6. o_____ to watch carefully the way sth. happens or the way sb. does sth., especially in order to learn more about it
7. r_____ a person who lives or has their home in a place
8. u_____ to use sth. in an effective way
9. a_____ to make sth. known or tell people about sth. officially
10. r_____ happening, done, or chosen by chance rather than according to a plan

Task 2 Complete the following sentences with the words and expressions from Task 1. Change the form if necessary.

1. The role of scientists is to _____ and describe the world, not to try to control it.
2. She had already sold everything of value that she _____.
3. Although she often disagreed with me, she was always _____.
4. Greenpeace works to _____ awareness of the dangers that threaten our planet today.
5. "The team has great _____ to win," declared the coach. "I've no doubts on that score."
6. The vitamins come in a form that is easily _____ by the body.
7. We asked a _____ sample of people what they thought.
8. The prime minister has _____ that public spending will be increased next year.
9. I didn't think his comments were very _____ at the time.
10. The local _____ were angry at the lack of parking spaces.

Task 3 Complete the following sentences with the words given in appropriate forms.

1. He _____ (create) a wonderful meal from very few ingredients.
2. He saw himself _____ (reflect) in the shop window.
3. There were at least three _____ (generation)—grandparents, parents and children—at the wedding.
4. My grandfather disapproved of _____ (display) emotion in public.
5. I have _____ (engage) a secretary to deal with all my paperwork.
6. In this business, the _____ (risk) and the rewards are both very high.
7. Research has _____ (demonstrate) that babies can recognize their mother's voice very soon after birth.
8. Skiing at 80 miles per hour _____ (require) total concentration.
9. The report recommends that more resources _____ (devote) to teaching four-year-olds.
10. He had a neatly _____ (fold) handkerchief in his jacket pocket.

Task 4 Rewrite the following sentences after the models.

Model 1: The work presented in a neat and professional manner. And it often goes above and beyond what was required initially.

→*Not only is* the work presented in a neat and professional manner, *but* it often goes above and beyond what was required initially.

1. He has a first-class brain. He is also a tremendously hard worker.

   _____

2. The poor man had been arrested. He had been sent to prison as well.

   _____

3. The professors have their own ideas on the matter. The students have theirs too.

   _____

4. She is a teacher. She is also a poet.

   _____

5. He spoke more correctly. And he spoke more easily.

   _____

Model 2: China's growing gig economy helped to cushion unemployment during the pandemic. It reflected the strengthening flexibility among the country's workers.

→China's growing gig economy helped to cushion unemployment during the pandemic, *reflecting* the strengthening flexibility among the country's workers.

1. An Act was passed. It gave the army extraordinary powers.

2. She wrote hurriedly. She didn't notice the spelling errors.

3. He has been courting the director. He hoped to get the leading role in the play.

4. She travelled widely throughout North America. She lectured on women's rights.

5. The little boy went upstairs. He trailed his teddy bear behind him.

Task 5 Translate the following sentences into English, using the given words or phrases.

1. Their 2-0 victory today has _____ (稳操胜券进入世界杯的决赛) for the Italian team. (ensure, the Cup Final)

2. She has _____ (将她全部的精力奉献给) the care of homeless people. (devote)

3. The government is _____ (为健康教育拨款4 000万元). (allocate, health education)

4. Offers of help _____ (源源不断地到达灾区) from all over the country. (flow)

5. Mexican farm workers _____ (大批涌入美国找工作) each year at harvest time. (migrate)

Applied writing

Request for leave (请假条)

请假条是用于向老师或上级请示不参加某项工作或学习活动的请示性文书，广泛运用于校园及工作场所。请假理由一般分为病假和事假两类。请假条中须包含请假人信息、请假事由、请假时间等信息，必要时亦可包含请假期间的学习计划或工作交接情况等。阅读下面的请假条样例，并指出其中的重要信息。

Sample

Request for leave

November 24, 2021

Dear Mr. Wang,

  My name is Li Ming and I am enrolled in your mathematics class. My student ID No. is 20200145. I would like to ask for a sick leave from your class today. Because I hurt my leg this morning when playing basketball and need to leave campus for hospital as soon as possible. I am really sorry for the absence and I will learn this session by myself and hand in the homework on time. Thank you very much for your consideration.

Yours sincerely,
Li Ming

Writing task

  Li Ming is going to participate in a public speaking contest next Wednesday. Since the competition is held in another city, he will need to leave the campus for three days. Suppose you are Li Ming, write a request letter to the department to ask for leave. You should write no less than 100 words.

Project performing

Work ethics and future profession

  This project aims to foster your understanding of work ethics with reference to your own future career choice. As we have discussed in this unit, work ethic is not a single trait, but a set of principles and skills related to work. In fact, these principles and skills may vary slightly across different professions. What's your dream job? What are the work ethics associated with it? In this project, you are required to work out the valuable features for a particular occupation in groups.

  The project is divided into three parts, preparation, presentation, and communication. Please follow the task description to complete the project step by step.

Unit 5 | Work Ethics and Job Security

Exercises

1. Preparation

(1) Get into small groups of 3 to 4 students;

(2) Decide on 2 or more occupations that your group members are interested in;

(3) Brainstorm and work out a list of principles that are considered to show a strong work ethic for each chosen occupation;

(4) Make a comparison between the work ethics of two different occupations.

2. Presentation

(1) Prepare a presentation to introduce the occupations you choose and the work ethics related to them. Make sure to include:

  A. A general description of each occupation;

  B. The work ethics associated with each occupation;

  C. The comparison between the work ethics of different occupations.

(2) Decide on the form of presentation. You can:

  A. Make up dialogues between employers and employees to present the occupations and their work ethics;

  B. Give a group presentation with every group member in charge of one part;

  C. Choose a representative to deliver the presentation but make sure that everyone makes contribution.

(3) Give the presentation in front of the class.

3. Communication

(1) Listen to other groups' presentation carefully and compare their occupations and the work ethics with yours;

(2) Exchange your ideas with other groups.

Conditional clause (条件句)

条件句是状语从句的一种,即由状语从句表示主句动作发生条件的主从复合句。

1. 分类

(1)真实条件句:所描述的事件是事实或在说话人看来可能实现的事情,多用于表达可能性预测、承诺、因果关系等。

(2)非真实条件句:条件与事实相反或不可能实现的事情,即虚拟语气,多用于表达假设、不可能情况、非真实情况、给出建议等。

2. 常用引导词

if(如果);unless(除非);once(一旦);in case(以防;万一);as/so long as(只要);provided/given that(假如);suppose/supposing that(假如)等。

If you cheat in the exam, you'll never get away with it. 考试作弊必予追究。

Unless you go at once, you will be late. 如果你不马上走,就会迟到。

I'll remember that day as long as I live. 只要我活着,我就不会忘记那个日子。

In case I forget, please remind me about it. 以防我忘记,请提醒我一下。

Once I know this, I will tell you. 一旦我知道了这件事,我就会告诉你。

3. 真实条件句中的主从句时态

从句时态	主句时态	例句
一般现在时:do/be	一般将来时:will do/be	If you don't study hard, you will fail the exam. 如果你不努力学习,你将会考不及格。
	情态动词:can/may/must/need/should do/be	He should see a doctor if he has a fever. 如果他发烧了,就应该去看医生。
	祈使语气:do/be	Please call me if he comes back. 如果他回家,请打电话给我。

4. 虚拟语气中的主从句时态

类型	从句时态	主句时态	例句
现在虚拟	一般过去时：did/were* (*所有人称和数均用were)	would/should/could/might do	If I were you, I would not throw the map away. 如果我是你，就不会扔掉地图。
过去虚拟	过去完成时：had done/been	would/should/could/might have done	If I had done it, I should have told you. 如果我做了，我应该就会告诉你。
将来虚拟	过去将来时：should do/were to do/did	would/should/could/might do	If he were to go home today, he would not come here tomorrow. 如果他今天回家，他明天就不会来这儿。

Task 1 Choose the best answer to complete the sentences.

1. They will go to the park _____ it is sunny tomorrow.
   A. when   B. while   C. if   D. whether

2. What should you do _____ you want to keep healthy?
   A. whether   B. why   C. unless   D. if

3. If he _____ harder, he will catch up with us soon.
   A. study   B. studies   C. will study   D. studied

4. Do you know if we will go to the cinema tomorrow? I think we'll go if we _____ too much homework.
   A. will have   B. had   C. won't have   D. don't have

5. If it _____ rain tomorrow, they'll go to the zoo.
   A. doesn't   B. won't   C. don't   D. isn't

6. If Mike _____ up earlier, he can finish the work in time.
   A. get   B. gets   C. will get   D. is getting

7. —Helen, do you know if Martin _____ to my party next week?
   —I think he will come if he _____ free.
   A. will come; will be   B. will come; is   C. come; is   D. comes; will be

8. I don't know if he _____ tomorrow. If he _____, we'll climb the mountain.
   A. comes; comes   B. comes; will come   C. will come; comes   D. will come; will come

9. Henry will give us a report as soon as he _____.
   A. arrives   B. arrived   C. is arriving   D. will arrive

10. Bill _____ a house if he had enough money.
    A. will buy   B. would buy   C. bought   D. has bought

Task 2 Complete the following sentences with the proper forms of the given verbs.

1. If I _____ (go) to the party, they _____ (be) upset.
2. If I _____ (take) a taxi, it _____ (be) too expensive.
3. If she _____ (finish) work early, she can go home.
4. If the weather is fine, we _____ (go) for a walk.
5. If I _____ (have) time tonight, I will finish the book.
6. If it _____ (rain) next Sunday, we won't be able to plant trees.
7. If she _____ (arrive) home, she will phone me.
8. Unless you speak to him first, she _____ (not speak) to you.
9. If he _____ (call) to you, tell him I will ring back.
10. Don't come unless I _____ (call) you.

Task 3 Rewrite the following sentences after the model.

Model 1: Work hard, and you will make your English better.
→ *If you work hard*, you will make your English better.

1. Help me, and I will help you, too.

2. Wear jeans, and the teacher won't let you in.

3. Go to the party, and we will have a great time.

4. Keep a secret, and I can tell you the truth.

Model 2: Work hard, or you will fail in the exam.
→ *If you don't work hard*, you will fail in the exam.

1. Keep quiet at the meeting, or you will have to leave.

2. Hurry up, or you'll miss the early train.

3. Buy a ticket, or you can't get into the park.

4. Don't forget to take an umbrella, or you will be caught in the rain.

Self-evaluation

Rate your own progress in this unit.	D	M	P	F*
I can say many words and expressions concerning work ethics and job security in English.	☐	☐	☐	☐
I can tell the traits that show a strong work ethic.	☐	☐	☐	☐
I can talk about the status quo of China's employment market.	☐	☐	☐	☐
I can talk about emerging professions and industries.	☐	☐	☐	☐
I can write an English request for leave.	☐	☐	☐	☐
I have mastered the conditional clause.	☐	☐	☐	☐

*Note: D (Distinction), M (Merit), P (Pass), F (Fail)

Culture

The digital divide between urban and rural areas

China has the world's biggest internet market with more than 904 million internet users as of March 2019, according to China Internet Network Information Centre (CNNIC), an agency under the Ministry of Industry and Information Technology. More than 90 percent of people under 18 years old have got online access in China.

However, there has been a digital divide between Chinese youth in urban and rural areas, which became all-too apparent when schools nationwide were forced to shut down, as the government tried to contain the spread of the coronavirus pandemic in 2020. Online learning was made compulsory, but that put many students living in remote areas at a disadvantage because they did not have sufficient internet access.

 Task 1 Watch the video clip and describe the main content of the video.

 Task 2 Make comments on the video and have a group discussion on the following topics.

1. How do you feel after watching the video clip?
2. What is Internet penetration rate?
3. What can we do to improve the situation?

Unit 6
Life-long Learning

Learning objectives

After studying this unit, you should be able to:
- get familiar with the words and expressions related to life-long learning;
- master how to use absolute construction;
- write letters of condolence;
- set up life goals and make life-long learning plans;
- have a positive attitude towards study and life.

Warm-up

Task 1 Watch the video twice and get the main idea of it.

Task 2 Watch the video once more and talk about the importance of life-long learning with your classmates.

Task 3 Look at the following pictures and discuss the following questions with your classmates. The phrases and expressions are for your reference.

1. Travel around the world   2. Become a dancer   3. Obtain a master's degree   4. Start my own business

---

A. study English

B. improve my communicative skills

C. learn management

D. study further and get a master's degree

E. get a diploma

F. change my major

G. pass the exam and get a permit

---

1. Do you have similar life goal(s)?
2. What are you going to do to meet your life goal(s)?

Reading A

Pre-reading questions
1. What is your understanding of life-long learning?
2. Why is it important to keep life-long learning?

Life-long learning amid ongoing change

China has made unprecedented investments to bring education to the younger generation over the past 30 years, but now faces a new challenge: ensuring the population has the skills to thrive in a fast-changing economy.

Today, 91 percent of secondary education teachers hold a Bachelor's degree or higher, up from only 24 percent in 2000. The number of college admissions soared to 9.1 million in 2019, from 3.7 million in 2000. Although gaps in quality and access must still be filled, the system meets the Chinese industrial economy's needs.

But China is rapidly evolving to an economy driven by consumption, services and innovation: a post-industrial economy. Transforming China's talent-development systems is necessary to turn the world's largest workforce into a nation of life-long learners.

Digital technologies and automation are on the rise, changing the skill types that will be in demand. Digitization and automation have accelerated amid COVID-19, therefore the need to reskill and potentially change occupations may have become even more urgent.

While demand for physical and manual skills could fall 18 percent in the period to 2030, demand for technological skills could rise by 51 percent. Up to 220 million Chinese workers—about 30 percent of the workforce—may need to change occupations by 2030. Particular attention must be paid to China's millions of migrant workers who tend to be low-skilled and low-paid with few resources for training.

China needs an ambitious plan for reskilling centered on the "three Es": everyone, everything and everywhere. Everyone needs access to training, notably the nation's 775 million workers. By 2030, that implies that the system should accommodate three times as many people enrolled in the education system today.

Content must offer everything—the broad capabilities that equip Chinese people for a fast-evolving economy, notably high cognitive skills (including critical thinking and decision-making), social and emotional skills (including interpersonal skills and leadership) and technical skills (including advanced data analysis) will be in demand. This requires investment in developing different content beyond traditional textbooks, including case studies and hands-on projects as well as new delivery approaches including participatory learning and experiential training.

Based on surveys of best practices in China and around the world, we identified four levers around which pilot projects can be designed to test what works and what does not.

First, digital technologies. Their adoption can enable more engaging multichannel learning and teaching. These technologies can empower content creators to deliver "micro curricula", and make content delivery more exciting and personalized by using tools including artificial intelligence, augmented and virtual reality, and gamification. More than 900 million people could benefit.

Second, a collaborative skills development ecosystem. Expanded public-private partnerships can help address the gap between workforce skills and employers' needs. Enterprises can play a more significant role in vocational education, the design of curricula, training and recruiting.

Third, an enhanced vocational education track. Workers need flexibility in returning to school, receiving retraining, and pursuing higher-skill jobs. China could create multiple entry points while making vocational education more attractive to prospective high school students, for instance by expanding a "3+4" model that enables them to go directly to application-oriented universities. Vocational trainers could collaborate more with companies to gain up-to-date knowledge, and more company representatives could come to vocational schools to teach.

Last, shifting attitudes and incentivizing change. Backing up such transformation requires changing attitudes—for everyone to "own" their life-long learning journeys by using information platforms and a micro-credential system to navigate career options and skills-development paths. Companies can strengthen the provision of training to develop their workers, potentially with government financial support in the form of co-funding or tax incentives.

China's continued prosperity and economic dynamism as well as its citizen's livelihoods hinge on wide-ranging reform to the nation's skills, and the work must start now. As the saying goes: "It takes 10 years to grow a tree, but 100 years to cultivate people."

(645 words)

New words

*unprecedented	/ʌnˈpresɪdentɪd/	a.	前所未有的；没有先例的
*investment	/ɪnˈvestmənt/	n.	投资
*challenge	/ˈtʃælɪndʒ/	n.	挑战
*economy	/ɪˈkɒnəmi/	n.	经济；经济制度；经济结构
*consumption	/kənˈsʌmpʃn/	n.	消耗；消费
▲innovation	/ˌɪnəˈveɪʃn/	n.	创造；创新；改革
▲accelerate	/əkˈseləreɪt/	v.	加快；加速
▲potentially	/pəˈtenʃəli/	ad.	潜在地

*manual	/ˈmænjuəl/	a.	手工的；体力的
*resource	/rɪˈsɔːs/	n.	资源；财力
*ambitious	/æmˈbɪʃəs/	a.	有野心的；有雄心的
*imply	/ɪmˈplaɪ/	v.	含有……的意思；暗示
▲cognitive	/ˈkɒɡnətɪv/	a.	认知的；感知的
*identify	/aɪˈdentɪfaɪ/	v.	确认；鉴定；找到；发现
lever	/ˈliːvə/	n.	（车辆或机器的）操纵杆；杠杆
multichannel	/ˈmʌltɪtʃænl/	a.	多频道的；多通道的
curricula	/kəˈrɪkjʊlə/	n.	课程（curriculum的复数）
▲augment	/ɔːɡˈment/	v.	增加；提高；扩大
▲collaborative	/kəˈlæbərətɪv/	a.	合作的；协作的；协力的
▲ecosystem	/ˈiːkəʊsɪstəm/	n.	生态系统
*enhance	/ɪnˈhɑːns/	v.	提高；增强；增进
▲prospective	/prəˈspektɪv/	a.	可能的；预期的；潜在的；即将发生
▲incentivize	/ɪnˈsentɪvaɪz/	v.	激励；以物质刺激鼓励
▲incentive	/ɪnˈsentɪv/	n.	激励；刺激；鼓励
▲prosperity	/prɒˈsperəti/	n.	繁荣；成功；昌盛；兴旺
▲livelihood	/ˈlaɪvlihʊd/	n.	赚钱谋生的手段；生计
▲hinge	/hɪndʒ/	v.	给（某物）装铰链

Phrases & expressions

on the rise	增加；提高；好转
in demand	很受欢迎；需求量大
as well as	及；既……又……；除……之外（也）
hinge on	取决于

生词数	生词率	*B级词汇	*A级词汇	▲四、六级词汇	超纲词汇
27	4.2%	5	7	12	3

Notes

1. Bachelor's degree

学士学位，是高等教育本科阶段授予的学位名称。它表示学位取得者较好地掌握了本门学科的基础理论、专业知识和基本技能，并具有从事科学研究工作或担负专门技术工作的初步能力。

2. digital technology

数字技术是指借助一定的设备将各种信息，包括图、文、声、像等，转化为电子计算机能识别的二进制数字"0"和"1"后进行运算、加工、存储、传送、传播、还原的技术。

3. automation

自动化主要研究电子技术、自动控制、系统工程、信息处理等方面的基本知识和技术，进行自动化系统的分析、设计、开发与研究，实现对各种装置和系统的自动控制。

4. migrant workers

外来务工人员；到城市工作的农民工

5. virtual reality

虚拟现实

6. application-oriented universities

应用型高等院校

7. It takes 10 years to grow a tree, but 100 years to cultivate people.

十年树木，百年树人

After-reading tasks

Task 1 Tick off the reasons why it is important for the workforce in China to become life-long learners according to Reading A.

☐ 1. demand technological skills ☐ 2. increasing demand for manual skills
☐ 3. change occupations ☐ 4. the influence of COVID-19
☐ 5. personal interests ☐ 6. post-industrial economy

Task 2 Read Reading A again and decide whether each of the following statement is true or false.

( ) 1. After 30 years, the younger generation in China has enough skills to thrive in a fast-changing economy.

( ) 2. Digitization and automation have slowed down amid COVID-19.

( ) 3. China should attract more high school students to go directly to application-oriented universities.

( ) 4. Digital technologies and automation are becoming less important during COVID-19.

( ) 5. Enterprises can play a more significant role in vocational education in the future.

Unit 6 | Life-long Learning 143

Listening and speaking

Task 1 Listen to the dialogue three times and choose the best answer.

1. What is most likely to be the relationship between the two speakers?
   A. Father and son.   B. Husband and wife.
   C. Teacher and student.   D. Shop assistant and customer.
2. How is Li Ming recently?
   A. Happy.   B. Relaxed.   C. Stressful.   D. Excited.
3. Why is Li Ming a bit worried?
   A. He has difficulty finding a job.
   B. He is preparing the exams but can't stay focused.
   C. He broke up with his girlfriend.
   D. He didn't pass the exam.
4. Which of the following is not the advice given by Mr. Zhang?
   A. Visiting a doctor.   B. Cooking a meal.
   C. Clean the room.   D. Washing clothes.
5. Which of the following is true according to the passage?
   A. Li Ming is in high spirits recently.
   B. Mr. Zhang Jun is in high spirits recently.
   C. Doing chores can be helpful to reduce pressure.
   D. Doing chores can add to pressure.

Task 2 Listen to the passage and number the steps to maintain your privacy in the right order.

(　　) A. check your privacy settings on your social media accounts
(　　) B. block cookies
(　　) C. don't put anything too private on your media accounts
(　　) D. change the default setting
(　　) E. deleting your browsing history

Task 3 Listen to the passage and fill in the blanks.

Summer vacation is coming. ___1___ a summer program is a good way to improve your skills and ___2___ new friends. The college has researched and collected the best summer activities for you.

The art farm

You are not a student. You are an ___3___! It offers small group studios led by professional artists. The ___4___ include glass, clay, metal, drawing and print-making. They are open from July 15th to July 19th 2021.

The music academy

The music academy ___5___ a creative and supportive environment for young adults to grow into musicians. The program offers rich music courses which are taught by teachers and top music educators from across the country. Our program this year is from July ___6___ to July 25th 2021.

Leadership program includes leadership exercises and speech ___7___. It will ___8___ young people's leadership skills. Our program this year will be held from July 26th to July 30th 2021.

Engineering experience

Have you ever wanted to build a ___9___ or program a robot? Join us for a hands-on program to the world of engineering. Student will use their design skills and scientific methods to ___10___ real engineering problems.

Task 4 Listen to the passage three times and answer the questions.

1. What is the basic definition of a habit?

2. According to a study, how long does it take to form a new habit?

3. Is willpower the most important thing people need to create a new habit?

4. How fast should we change things when trying to create a new habit?

Task 5 Make up a dialogue and talk about how to form a good study habit. The expressions given below are for your reference.

- Can you give me some advice?
- I play video games all the time.
- I sometimes study for a whole day, but I can't focus on my study most of the time.
- Take your time. Don't change too much at once.
- Make a list of things to do on a piece of paper.
- Put study (reading, writing or doing homework) on top of the list.
- Do the most important thing first.
- Try to keep a good mood.
- Give yourself a little gift if you make progress.
- If you fail, don't lose your heart.
- Start again.

Task 6 The following are the benefits of keeping life-long learning. Please choose the top 3, and explain your ideas to your partners why you think they are the most important ones.

- Enhance your career.
- Enrich your life.
- Update your skills.
- Keep your mind sharp.
- Set a good example for your kid.
- Keep healthy.
- Enter a fast track to success.
- Make friends.

Life-long learning

Most people associate learning with formal education at school, college, university, etc. We are all told, from an early age, that we should get a good education. Education may maximize our potential to find better, more satisfying jobs, earn more and, perhaps, become more successful in our chosen career.

However, schooling is only one type of learning. There are many other opportunities to further your knowledge and develop the skills you need throughout life.

Knowledge can be acquired and skills developed anywhere—learning is unavoidable and happens all the time. However, life-long learning is about creating and maintaining a positive attitude to learning both for personal and professional development. Life-long learners are motivated to learn and develop because they want to: it is a deliberate and voluntary act.

Learning for personal development

Keeping the brain active does have advantages since learning can prevent you from becoming bored and thus enable a more fulfilling life at any age.

There are many reasons why people learn for personal development.

- You may want to increase your knowledge or skills around a particular hobby or pastime that you enjoy.
- Perhaps you want to develop some entirely new skill that will in some way enhance your life—take a pottery or car mechanic course for example.
- Perhaps you want to research a medical condition or your ancestry.
- Perhaps you're planning a trip and want to learn more about the history and culture of your destination.
- Maybe you will decide to take a degree course later in life simply because you enjoy your chosen subject and the challenges of academic study.

Learning for professional development

Although qualifications may get you an interview, actually getting the job can take a lot more. Employers are looking for well-balanced people with transferable skills. This includes the ability to be able to demonstrate that you are keen to learn and develop.

While you are employed, take advantage of training, coaching or mentoring opportunities and work on your continuous professional development as you will likely become better at what you do and more indispensable to your current or future employer.

We can get more personal satisfaction from our lives and jobs as we understand more about who we are and what we do. This can lead to better results and a more rewarding working day in turn.

From a financial point of view, a more highly skilled and knowledgeable worker is an asset to any company and can lead to faster promotion with associated salary increases.

Someone who can offer more expertise will be of more value not just to employers but also to customers. Expertise is also, often, a key quality of an effective leader.

Learning gives you options

The bottom line is that, whatever your life path, there are a number of sometimes unanticipated benefits to continual personal and professional development.

Whatever your age, it's never too late to start.

Successfully changing career path in mid-life and spending time informally developing expertise is more common than ever, especially during rapidly changing market conditions.

Our economy is shifting increasingly towards short-term and part-time contracts with more flexible work-patterns whilst old industries are shifting abroad. We have to adapt to changes going on in the work-world and make more of ourselves by stepping out of our comfort zones and ideas of how we believe our life is going.

Because of work-life instability, more people of all ages are turning their hobby into a business idea. Continually following one's passion outside of work hours can lead you to get paid for doing what you love, and typically you will develop business and other transferable skills as you go along until the point that you can delegate your least favourite jobs.

(623 words)

New words

*maximize	/ˈmæksɪmaɪz/	v.	充分利用；最大限度地利用
*acquire	/əˈkwaɪə(r)/	v.	获得
unavoidable	/ˌʌnəˈvɔɪdəbl/	a.	无法避免的；难以预防的
▲deliberate	/dɪˈlɪbərət/	a.	故意的；蓄意的；存心的；深思熟虑的
▲voluntary	/ˈvɒləntri/	a.	自愿的
▲ancestry	/ˈænsestri/	n.	世系；血统
transferable	/trænsˈfɜːrəbl/	a.	可转移的；可转换的
▲indispensable	/ˌɪndɪˈspensəbl/	a.	不可或缺的
▲asset	/ˈæset/	n.	有价值的人（或事物）；资产；财产
▲expertise	/ˌekspɜːˈtiːz/	n.	专门知识；专门技能；专长
▲option	/ˈɒpʃn/	n.	选择；选择权；选择的自由
unanticipated	/ˌʌnænˈtɪsɪpeɪtɪd/	a.	没想到的；未预料到的
*delegate	/ˈdelɪɡeɪt/	v.	把（工作等）委托（给下级）

Phrases & expressions

associate sth. with sth.	把两者联系在一起
be motivated to	有动机有积极性做某事
prevent sb. from doing sth.	阻止某人做某事

生词数	生词率	*B级词汇	*A级词汇	▲四、六级词汇	超纲词汇
13	2.1%	0	3	7	3

Notes

1. the bottom line
底线,通常指最低的条件或最低的限度。

2. comfort zone
舒适区,又称为心理舒适区,指的是一个人所表现的心理状态和习惯性的行为模式,人会在这种状态或模式中感到舒适。

After-reading tasks

Task 1 Complete the mindmap based on your understanding of Reading B.

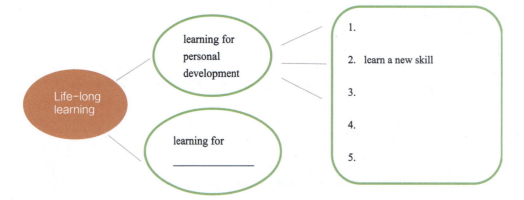

Task 2 Translate the following paragraph into Chinese.

Our economy is shifting increasingly towards short-term and part-time contracts with more flexible work-patterns whilst old industries are shifting abroad. We have to adapt to changes going on in the work-world and make more of ourselves by stepping out of our comfort zones and ideas of how we believe our life is going.

Unit 6 | Life-long Learning

Comprehensive exercises

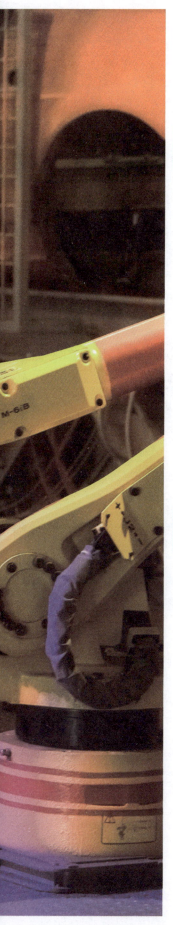

Task 1 Fill in the blanks with the words or expressions from Reading A and Reading B that match the meanings in the column on the right. The first letters are given.

1. e_____ the system according to which the money, industry, and trade of a country or region are organized
2. m_____ doing physical work that requires use of the hands
3. i_____ determine the identity of
4. e_____ to raise to a higher degree; intensify; magnify
5. f_____ the ability to change or be changed easily
6. p_____ being successful and having a lot of money
7. c_____ to cause difficulties for someone or something
8. e_____ to make something certain to happen
9. o_____ one of the choices or decisions one can make
10. d_____ to show or make something clear

Task 2 Complete the following sentences with the words and expressions from Task 1. Change the form if necessary.

1. Schools in China must meet the _____ of new technology.
2. School staff and people in the community acted swiftly to _____ the safety of the students.
3. Employees must _____ competence in certain skills before they can work independently.
4. The primary goal of the local government was to support sustainable economic growth and _____ in the region.
5. She learnt to _____ medical herbs from a local farmer.
6. Most _____ labor in the past has been replaced by modern machines.
7. As a professor with more _____ than his wife, Jonathan is more involved in taking care of their daughter.
8. He had no _____ but to agree.
9. COVID-19 has caused serious damage to the country's _____ .
10. Good communicative skills will _____ your opportunities of getting a job.

Task 3 Fill in the blanks with the words given in appropriate forms.

1. What do you assume is the minimum and _____ (maximize) capacity of the new car?
2. Mary has to gave up her apartment in town and move to the countryside because of _____ (economy) considerations.
3. She now helps in a local school as a _____ (voluntary) three days a week.
4. You had better _____ (unavoidable) reading in a moving vehicle.
5. He found he could no longer cope with that _____ (demand) job.

Task 4 Rewrite the following sentences after the model.

Model 1: People's work and life are instable. More people are turning their hobby into a business idea.
→ *Because of* work-life instability, more people are turning their hobby into a business idea.

1. It is very cold.
   We stayed indoors.
   _____

2. She was exposed to radiation.
   She developed blood cancer.
   _____

Model 2: *No matter* how old you are, it's never too late to start.
→*Whatever* your age, it's never too late to start.

1. The centre is open to all, *no matter* who they are, men and women, young and old.
   _____

2. She is shadowed by detectives *no matter* where she goes.
   _____

Task 5 Translate the following sentences into English, using the given words or phrases.

1. 这孩子既健康又活泼。(as well as)

2. 夏季冷饮的需求很大。(in demand)

3. 他是出自爱心,并不指望得到任何汇报。(be motivated)

4. 年轻人离开学校以后,职业顾问和他们保持联系。(maintain)

5. 他是个很有抱负的小伙子,想参加最高水平的比赛。(ambitious)

Applied writing

Letter of condolence (慰问信)

当亲友生病、受伤、去世，或遭遇灾害、意外事故等而蒙受不幸时，我们就应该给他们写封信表示慰问。首先，要对他们的遭遇表示同情和安慰；其次，表达提供帮助的意愿；最后，以真挚的希望、同情或安慰结束信件。

Sample

Letter of condolence

August 30, 2021

Dear Mrs. Smith,

  I was very shocked to hear the death of Mr. Smith. Please accept my sincerest sympathy on this terrible loss. I will always remember Mr. Smith for his wonderful sense of humor, and the help and care he gave to me.

  I sincerely admire how competent you were in providing excellent care for Mr. Smith as his health declined. I was impressed by your devotion to him.

  I've sent to you some photos of Mr. Smith taken in the work place. My colleagues and I all miss him very much! I'll phone you to see how you are doing and what I can do for you.

  My thoughts are with you and your family at this sad moment.

Yours sincerely,

Li Ming

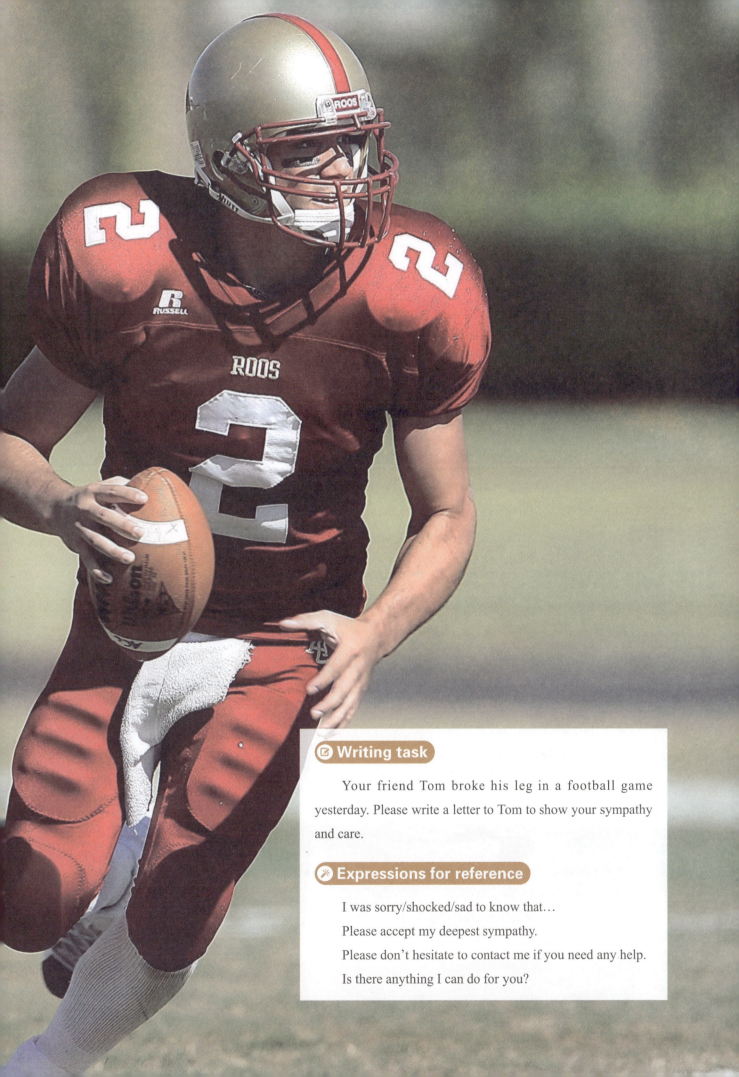

Writing task

Your friend Tom broke his leg in a football game yesterday. Please write a letter to Tom to show your sympathy and care.

Expressions for reference

I was sorry/shocked/sad to know that…
Please accept my deepest sympathy.
Please don't hesitate to contact me if you need any help.
Is there anything I can do for you?

Project performing

Career development plan (职业规划)

When making your career development plan, you should think about the four points:

1. The starting point

Where you are now in your career development plan

2. The destination

Your objectives in 5 years or in 10 years, for example

3. The gap

The obstacles you must overcome to reach the destination

4. The route

How to close the gap to reach your intended destination

Guidelines

This project aims to enhance your understanding of life-long learning and encourage you to make your career development plan. Please follow the task description to complete the project.

1. Group discussion

(1) Work in small groups of 3 to 4 students;

(2) Talk about your dream job(s);

(3) Brainstorm and work out a list of skills that is needed for the occupation;

(4) Share your ideas within the group.

2. Presentation

(1) Volunteers give presentations to the whole class.

(2) Introduce an occupation and the skills needed. Make sure to include:

- A general description of the occupation;
- The skills that are needed;
- How to learn the skills;
- How to overcome obstacles if there are any.

3. Communication and composition

(1) Discuss with your teacher and classmates the solutions to common obstacles.

(2) After discussion, write down your plans and try to carry them out.

Grammar

Absolute construction (独立主格结构)

独立主格结构是英语中的一种特殊结构。在英语中任何一个句子都要有主谓结构，而在独立主格结构中，没有真正的主语和谓语动词，但又在逻辑上构成主谓关系。独立主格的常见的形式和用法如下：

1. 形式

独立主格结构通常由名词或代词作为逻辑主语，加上分词、形容词、副词、动词不定式或介词短语作为逻辑谓语。这种结构在形式上与主句没有关系，所以称为"独立主格结构"。

2. 功能

独立主格结构的功能相当于一个状语从句，常用来表示时间、原因、条件、行为方式或伴随情况等。

3. 独立主格结构常见用法,形式和例句

用作	形式	例句
时间状语	名词/主格代词+过去分词（表示被动和已完成）	The work done (=After the work had been done), we went home. 工作完成后,我们就回家了。
条件状语	名词/主格代词+现在分词（表示主动）	Weather permitting (=If weather permits), we will go on an outing to the beach tomorrow. 如果天气允许的话,我们明天去海滨游玩。
伴随状语	with+名词/代词+介词短语	He stood at the door, with a computer in his hand. /He stood at the door, computer in hand. 他站在门口,手里拿着一部电脑。
补充说明	1. 名词/主格代词+现在分词,（表示补充说明,相当于一个并列句）。 2. 名词/主格代词+不定式（表示即将发生的动作）	1. We redoubled our efforts, each man working like two. 我们加倍努力,一个人干两个人的活。 2. They said good-bye to each other, one to go to school, the other to go to the bookstore. 他们道别后,一个去学校,一个去了书店。
原因状语	1. 名词/主格代词+不定式（表示即将发生的动作） 2. It being +名词（代词)	1. An important lecture to be given tomorrow (=As an important lecture will be given tomorrow), I have to stay up late into the night. 因为明天要发表一个重要的演讲,我不得不熬夜到很晚。 2. It being a holiday, all the shops were shut. 由于是假日,所有商店都关门了。

Task Complete the following sentences with the the given words in proper forms.

1. Time _____ (permit), I'll visit the Palace Museum.
2. _____ (walk) on the street, I run into an old friend.
3. I put on my coat, _____ (wear) the inside out.
4. An important essay _____ (write) tonight, I'll not go to the cinema.
5. The girl drove her car and _____ (wave) goodbye to her hero, with tears in in her eyes.
6. No one _____ (help) me, I may fail the exam.
7. Weather _____ (permit), we plan to climb the mountain.
8. With all my work _____ (do), I feel so relaxed and happy.
9. Mike was in a great hurry this morning, _____ (eat) a hamburger on his way to work.
10. The class is dismissed, the teacher _____ (catch) the train, the student to have their lunch.

Self-evaluation

Rate your own progress in this unit.	D	M	P	F*
I can list reasons for life-long learning.	☐	☐	☐	☐
I can talk about the economy and job market in China.	☐	☐	☐	☐
I can make a self-development plan.	☐	☐	☐	☐
I can write a letter of condolence in English.	☐	☐	☐	☐
I have mastered the absolute construction.	☐	☐	☐	☐

*Note: D (Distinction), M (Merit), P (Pass), F (Fail)

Unit 6 | Life-long Learning

Culture

Compliments are a part of everyday communication in the workplace. Many people use compliments to show approval, solidarity or interest in further developing a relationship. However, the way that compliments are given or interpreted as well as the frequency of using them may vary from culture to culture, and from person to person.

Task 1 Number the following topics in the order you have heard in the dialogue.

(   ) The woman's professional skills.
(   ) What the man can smell.
(   ) A business agreement.
(   ) The woman's fashion sense.
(   ) The woman's clothes.
(   ) A visit to the hairdresser.

Task 2 Discuss the following questions in groups.

1. Do you think the man has paid too much compliments to the woman?
2. How easy do you find it to pay someone a compliment?
3. How do you usually respond to a compliment?

New words & expressions

Unit 1

Reading A

New words

*category	/ˈkætəgəri/	n. (人或事物的)类别,种类	*vital	/ˈvaɪtl/	a. 必不可少的;对……极重要的;充满生机的
*staple	/ˈsteɪpl/	a. 主要的;基本的;重要的	*nutritional	/njuˈtrɪʃənl/	a. (食物中)营养的,营养成分的
*prevalent	/ˈprevələnt/	a. 流行的;普遍存在的;盛行的	*property	/ˈprɒpəti/	n. 所有物;财产;不动产
sustenance	/ˈsʌstənəns/	n. 食物;营养;养料	▲therapy	/ˈθerəpi/	n. 治疗;疗法
*ingredient	/ɪnˈɡriːdiənt/	n. 成分;(尤指烹饪)原料	*diet	/ˈdaɪət/	n. 日常饮食;规定饮食(为健康或减肥等目的)
▲authentic	/ɔːˈθentɪk/	a. 真正的;真实的;逼真的			v. 节食;按规定饮食
▲fusion	/ˈfjuːʒn/	n. 融合;熔接;结合	*influence	/ˈɪnfluəns/	n. 影响;作用;有影响的人(或事物)
aroma	/əˈrəʊmə/	n. 芳香;香味			v. 影响;对……起作用;支配;左右
aesthetic	/iːsˈθetɪk/	n. (审)美学;美的哲学	ailment	/ˈeɪlmənt/	n. 轻病;小恙
▲utensil	/juːˈtensl/	n. (家庭)用具,器皿	*treat	/triːt/	v. 处理;治疗;把……看作
wok	/wɒk/	n. 炒菜锅	*avoid	/əˈvɔɪd/	v. 避免;防止;躲避
*essential	/ɪˈsenʃl/	a. 必要的;必不可少的;根本的	*herb	/hɜːb/	n. 药草;香草;草本植物
		n. 必不可少的东西;必需品;要点	▲absorb	/əbˈzɔːb/	v. 吸收(液体、气体等)
▲integral	/ˈɪntɪɡrəl/	a. 必需的;不可或缺的;整体			
		n. 整体			

*prevent /prɪˈvent/	v.	阻止；阻碍；阻挠	toxic /ˈtɒksɪk/	a.	有毒的；引起中毒的
*cure /kjʊə(r)/	v.	治愈，治好（疾病）；解决（问题）		n.	毒物；毒剂
	n.	药物；疗法；治疗			

Phrases & expressions

consist of	由……组成	in addition to	加之；另外；又
be divided by	按……划分	be infused with	融入

Reading B

New words

*calendar /ˈkælɪndə(r)/	n.	日历；挂历；日程表	*appetizer /ˈæpɪtaɪzə(r)/	n.	（餐前的）开胃品，开胃饮料
*region /ˈriːdʒən/	n.	地区，区域，地方；行政	*snack /snæk/	n.	点心；小吃；快餐
*significant /sɪɡˈnɪfɪkənt/	a.	有重大意义的；显著的	wrap /ræp/	n.	包裹（或包装）材料
Sinophone /ˈsaɪnəʊfəʊn/	n.	华语语系；译意风		v.	包；裹；用……包裹（或包扎、覆盖等）
*myth /mɪθ/	n.	神话	shiitake /ʃɪˈtɑːki/	n.	香菇；香蕈
*occasion /əˈkeɪʒn/	n.	场合；特别的事情（或仪式、庆典）	*seasoning /ˈsiːzənɪŋ/	n.	调味品；作料
*annual /ˈænjuəl/	a.	每年的；一年一次的；年度的	▲equivalent /ɪˈkwɪvələnt/	a.	（价值、数量、意义、重要性等）相等的，相同的
*reunion /ˌriːˈjuːniən/	n.	重逢；团聚；聚会；相聚；团圆	▲bonding /ˈbɒndɪŋ/	n.	人与人之间的关系
*decoration /ˌdekəˈreɪʃn/	n.	装饰品；装饰图案；装饰风格		v.	使……结合；使……联结
couplet /ˈkʌplət/	n.	对句（相连的两行长度相等的诗句）；对联	participate /pɑːˈtɪsɪpeɪt/	v.	参加；参与
			*Mandarin /ˈmændərɪn/	n.	（中文）普通话
			*longevity /lɒnˈdʒevəti/	n.	长寿；长命；持久
*firecracker /ˈfaɪəkrækə(r)/	n.	鞭炮；爆竹	*flexibility /ˌfleksəˈbɪləti/	n.	柔韧性；灵活性；弹性
*envelope /ˈenvələʊp/	n.	信封；塑料封套；塑料封皮	*symbolic /sɪmˈbɒlɪk/	a.	作为象征的；象征性的
*appear /əˈpɪə(r)/	v.	显得；看来；似乎；出现；呈现；显现	*loyalty /ˈlɔɪəlti/	n.	忠诚；忠实；忠心耿耿

*surplus /ˈsɜːpləs/	n.	过剩；剩余；盈余	*entire /ɪnˈtaɪə(r)/	a. 全部的；整个的；完全的
	a.	过剩的；剩余的；多余的	*auspicious /ɔːˈspɪʃəs/	a. 吉利的；吉祥的
*prolong /prəˈlɒŋ/	v.	延长	*claw /klɔː/	n. （动物或禽类的）爪；（水生有壳动物的）钳
*prosperous /ˈprɒspərəs/	a.	繁荣的；成功的；兴旺的		
*represent /ˌreprɪˈzent/	v.	代表；作为……的代言人	*ancestor /ˈænsestə(r)/	n. 祖宗；祖先
			*bubble /ˈbʌbl/	v. 起泡，冒泡
*harmonious /hɑːˈməʊniəs/			*broth /brɒθ/	n. （加入蔬菜的）肉汤，鱼汤
	a.	友好和睦的；和谐的；协调的	*dip /dɪp/	v. 蘸；浸
*protein /ˈprəʊtiːn/	n.	蛋白质		

💬 Phrases & expressions

be associated with	与……相关；与……联系	sweep away	扫清；肃清；冲走
		make way for	为……开路
be regarded as	被认为是；被当作是；视为		

Unit 2

Reading A

📖 New words

*etiquette /ˈetɪkət/	n. 礼仪；（社会或行业中的）礼节；规矩	*correspondence /ˌkɒrəˈspɒndəns/	n. 通信；相似
		*error /ˈerə(r)/	n. 错误；差错；谬误
*internship /ˈɪntɜːnʃɪp/	n. （学生或毕业生的）实习期	*permanent /ˈpɜːmənənt/	a. 永久的；永恒的
		*policy /ˈpɒləsi/	n. 政策；方针
*crucial /ˈkruːʃl/	a. 关键的	discern /dɪˈsɜːn/	v. 辨别；了解
*positive /ˈpɒzətɪv/	a. 积极乐观的	*division /dɪˈvɪʒn/	n. 部门；分开
*impression /ɪmˈpreʃn/	n. 印象；效果	navigate /ˈnævɪgeɪt/	v. 导航；找到正确方法
*perceive /pəˈsiːv/	v. 感知；将……理解为		
		professionalism /prəˈfeʃənəlɪzəm/	n. 专业水平；专业素质
*negatively /ˈneɡətɪvli/	ad. 消极的；负面的		
*frustrate /frʌˈstreɪt/	v. 使沮丧		
*subordinate /səˈbɔːdɪnət/	n. 下级；部属	cautious /ˈkɔːʃəs/	a. 小心的；谨慎的

*reflection /rɪˈflekʃn/	n.	反射;显示;表达	*schedule /ˈʃeduːl/	v. 安排;为……安排时间
*presence /ˈprezns/	n.	存在;出现		

Phrases & expressions

under one's belt	已有的经验和阅历（俚语）	dress code	着装要求
		interact with	互动
present oneself	展现自我	be mindful of	注意,留心
be aware of	意识到,知道	in regard to	至于,关于
make sure	确保,确信	be respectful of	尊重他人

Reading B

New words

*considerably /kənˈsɪdərəbli/	ad.	非常;很;相当多地	▲premise /ˈpremɪs/	n.	（企业或机构使用的）房屋及土地;经营场所
▲nuance /ˈnuːɑːns/	n.	细微的差别	▲limp /lɪmp/	a.	无力的;柔软的
▲solely /ˈsəʊlli/	ad.	唯一地	*approach /əˈprəʊtʃ/	v.	靠近;接近
*commitment /kəˈmɪtmənt/	n.	承诺	*acknowledge /əkˈnɒlɪdʒ/	v.	承认;搭理
			fix /fɪks/	n.	（尤指由自己引起的）困境,窘境
▲established /ɪˈstæblɪʃt/	a.	已确立的			
▲attire /əˈtaɪə(r)/	n.	服装	*individual /ˌɪndɪˈvɪdʒuəl/	n.	个人
*acceptable /əkˈseptəbl/	a.	（社会上）认同的,认可的;可接受的	*deliver /dɪˈlɪvə/	v.	发表
			*organizational /ˌɔːɡənaɪˈzeɪʃnəl/	a.	组织的;机构的
*wrinkle /ˈrɪŋkl/	n.	（尤指脸上的）皱纹	▲hierarchy /ˈhaɪərɑːki/	n.	等级制度（尤指社会或组织）
*suits /suːts/	n.	西服;套装			
▲tuxedo /tʌkˈsiːdəʊ/	n.	燕尾服	▲foul /faʊl/	a.	很令人不快的;下流的
*casual /ˈkæʒuəl/	a.	随便的,非正式的			
deviate /ˈdiːvieɪt/	v.	偏离;违背	▲racial /ˈreɪʃl/	a.	种族的;种族间的;人种的
*requirement /rɪˈkwaɪəmənt/	n.	要求;必要条件	▲sexist /ˈseksɪst/	n.	性别歧视者
*punctuality /ˌpʌŋktʃuˈæləti/	n.	准时	▲tipsy /ˈtɪpsi/	a.	略有醉意的
			*observe /əbˈzɜːv/	v.	注意到;观察到
*associate /əˈsəʊsieɪt/	n.	同事;伙伴;合伙人	*toast /təʊst/	n.	敬酒;祝酒

Phrases & expressions

seal a deal	达成交易	couple with	与……连接在一起；相伴随
refer to	查阅，提及		
according to	根据	in case	万一；假使
concentrate on	专注于		

Unit 3

Reading A

New words

intangible /ɪnˈtændʒəbl/	a. 无形的	*guarantee /ˌɡærənˈtiː/	v. 保证；担保
▲representation /ˌreprɪzenˈteɪʃn/	n. 表现	continuity /ˌkɒntɪˈnjuːəti/	n. 连续性；持续性
		sustainable /səˈsteɪnəbl/	a. 可持续的
*process /ˈprəʊses/	n. 过程；进程	momentum /məˈmentəm/	n. 动力；势头
*preserve /prɪˈzɜːv/	v. 保存，保留	nomination /ˌnɒmɪˈneɪʃn/	n. 提名；推荐
▲craft /krɑːft/	n. 手艺；工艺	*oral /ˈɔːrəl/	a. 口头的
*cuisine /kwɪˈziːn/	n. 烹饪；风味	▲interpretation /ɪnˌtɜːprəˈteɪʃn/	n. 理解；解释
artifact /ˈɑːtɪfækt/	n. 手工制品，手工艺品	genre /ˈʒɑːnrə/	n.（文学、艺术、电影或音乐的）体裁，类型
*vehicle /ˈviːəkl/	n. 手段，工具		
recreate /ˌriːkriˈeɪt/	v. 再现；再创造	*celebration /ˌselɪˈbreɪʃn/	n. 庆典；庆祝
▲surroundings /səˈraʊndɪŋz/	n. 周围的环境	ritual /ˈrɪtʃuəl/	a. 庆典的
▲grant /ɡrɑːnt/	v. 准予，允许	▲sophisticated /səˈfɪstɪkeɪtɪd/	a. 复杂的；水平高的
▲stability /stəˈbɪləti/	n. 稳定性	inventory /ˈɪnvəntri/	n. 库存
*unique /juˈniːk/	a. 唯一的；独特的	▲territory /ˈterətri/	n. 领土；版图
▲admiration /ˌædməˈreɪʃn/	n. 钦佩	▲maintain /meɪnˈteɪn/	v. 维持；保持
diversity /daɪˈvɜːsəti/	n. 多样化		

Phrases & expressions

recognize as	承认	based on	在……基础上
pass down	传递，传承	a variety of	各种各样的
define as	界定；定义为	associated with	与……有关
in response to	作为回应	result in	导致
interaction with	与……相互作用	take effect	生效
submit to	呈交		

Reading B

New words

▲impact /ˈɪmpækt/	n.	巨大影响	thrive /θraɪv/	v.	兴旺发达；繁荣
pandemic /pænˈdemɪk/	n.	流行病	testimony /ˈtestɪməni/	n.	证据；证明
*far-reaching /ˌfɑːˈriːtʃɪŋ/	a.	深远的	▲summarize /ˈsʌməraɪz/	v.	总结；概括；概述
devastating /ˈdevəsteɪtɪŋ/	a.	毁灭性的	▲crisis /ˈkraɪsɪs/	n.	危机
interconnectedness /ˌɪntəkəˈnektɪdnəs/	n.	关联性	▲mobilize /ˈməʊbəlaɪz/	v.	调动；调用
resilience /rɪˈzɪliəns/	n.	恢复力；弹力；适应力	*spark /spɑːk/	v.	引发；触发
▲psychological /ˌsaɪkəˈlɒdʒɪkl/	a.	心理的	insight /ˈɪnsaɪt/	n.	洞察力
▲unexpected /ˌʌnɪkˈspektɪd/	a.	出乎意料的；始料不及的	mechanism /ˈmekənɪzəm/	n.	方法；机制
*reliance /rɪˈlaɪəns/	n.	依赖	visibility /ˌvɪzəˈbɪləti/	n.	可见度
▲transmit /trænzˈmɪt/	v.	传输	amplify /ˈæmplɪfaɪ/	v.	放大，增强
▲restriction /rɪˈstrɪkʃn/	n.	限制	▲safeguard /ˈseɪfɡɑːd/	v.	保护；保障；捍卫
▲counter /ˈkaʊntə(r)/	v.	抵制；抵消	▲emergency /ɪˈmɜːdʒənsi/	n.	突发事件；紧急情况
			*preparedness /prɪˈpeərɪdnəs/	n.	（尤指对战争或灾难）有准备，做好准备

Phrases & expressions

highlight the importance of	强调……的重要性	attach importance to	重视
common humanity	共同的人道主义精神，共同的人性	thanks to	幸亏；归因于
struggle with	与……作斗争	in the midst of	在……当中
recover from	从……恢复	contribute to	有助于；促成
adapt... to...	使……适应……	integrate... into...	与……成为一体
put in place	就位，启用	take advantage of	利用

Unit 4

Reading A

New words

*surge /sɜːdʒ/	n.	激增	▲powerhouse /ˈpaʊəhaʊs/	n.	强国
*generation /ˌdʒenəˈreɪʃn/	n.	世，代，辈	*appeal /əˈpiːl/	n.	吸引力，魅力

*passionate /ˈpæʃənət/	a. 热情的，狂热的	*rebranding /ˌriːˈbrændɪŋ/	n. 重塑形象
▲demographic /ˌdeməˈgræfɪk/		nostalgia /nɒˈstældʒə/	n. 怀旧；恋旧
	n.（尤指特定年龄段的）人群	guerilla /gəˈrɪlə/	n. 游击队
		▲resurgence /rɪˈsɜːdʒəns/	n. 复苏

Phrases & expressions

known as	被称为	out of nowhere	突然出现
be confident about	对……有信心	be achieving with	用……达到
appeal to	对……有吸引力	be popular among	受……欢迎
outside of fashion	与时尚无关	due to	由于

Reading B

New words

▲inferior /ɪnˈfɪərɪə/	a. 差的，低等的	▲attribute /ˈætrɪˌbjuːt/	n. 特征，特性，属性
▲atmosphere /ˈætməsfɪə(r)/		*mechanically /mɪˈkænɪkli/	
	n. 气氛；氛围		ad. 使用机械地；机动地；在机械方面；机械上；机械地
▲prominent /ˈprɒmɪnənt/	a. 突出的，显著的		
enlightenment /ɪnˈlaɪtənmənt/		integration /ˌɪntɪˈgreɪʃn/	n. 结合；集成；一体化；整合
	n. 启蒙		
▲embark /ɪmˈbɑːk/	v. 登上		
rejuvenation /rɪˌdʒuːvəˈneɪʃən/		▲radiate /ˈreɪdɪˌeɪt/	v. 辐射；发散；从中心发散；呈辐射状发出
	n. 复兴		
profundity /prəˈfʌndɪtɪ/	n. 深度		
▲dispute /ˈdɪspjuːt/	n. 纠纷，争端	*vitality /vaɪˈtælətɪ/	n. 活力；生机；生命力；生存力
▲patriotism /ˈpeɪtrɪətɪzəm/			
	n. 爱国主义	▲ideological /ˌaɪdɪəˈlɒdʒɪkl/	
connotation /ˌkɒnəˈteɪʃən/	n. 内涵		a. 思想观念上的；思想体系的；意识形态的
*practicability /ˌpræktɪkəˈbɪlɪtɪ/			
	n. 实用性，可行性		

Phrases & expressions

be inferior to	不如	so as to	以便
under the influence of	在……的影响下	as long as	只要
be eager to	渴望		

Unit 5

Reading A

New words

ethic /ˈeθɪk/	n.	道德；伦理；行为准则
possess /pəˈzes/	v.	拥有，具有
trait /treɪt/	n.	特征，特性，品质
require /rɪˈkwaɪə(r)/	v.	需要；要求
oversight /ˈəʊvəsaɪt/	n.	监督；监察；监管
manager /ˈmænɪdʒə(r)/	n.	经理；主管
complete /kəmˈpliːt/	v.	完成；完工；使完整
factor /ˈfæktə(r)/	n.	因素；要素
demonstrate /ˈdemənstreɪt/	v.	显示；表明
behave /bɪˈheɪv/	v.	行事，表现
shift /ʃɪft/	n.	班；轮班
courteous /ˈkɜːtiəs/	a.	有礼貌的；谦恭有礼的
random /ˈrændəm/	a.	任意的；随机的；胡乱的
authorization /ˌɔːθəraɪˈzeɪʃn/	n.	批准，准许；授权
consistent /kənˈsɪstənt/	a.	一贯的；坚持的；始终如一的
devote /dɪˈvəʊt/	v.	将……贡献给，把……奉献给
proposal /prəˈpəʊzl/	n.	建议；计划；提案
administrative /ədˈmɪnɪstrətɪv/	a.	管理的；行政的
productivity /ˌprɒdʌkˈtɪvəti/	n.	生产力；生产率；生产能力
foster /ˈfɒstə(r)/	v.	促进；鼓励
ensure /ɪnˈʃʊə(r)/	v.	确保；保证
internal /ɪnˈtɜːnl/	a.	内部的，内在的
motivation /ˌməʊtɪˈveɪʃn/	n.	积极性，干劲；动机，诱因
issue /ˈɪʃuː/	n.	问题；议题
frustration /frʌˈstreɪʃn/	n.	挫折；沮丧
remedy /ˈremədi/	n.	补救办法；疗法
determination /dɪˌtɜːmɪˈneɪʃn/	n.	决心；毅力
permeate /ˈpɜːmieɪt/	v.	渗透；弥漫；遍布；充满
manner /ˈmænə(r)/	n.	方式，方法
beyond /bɪˈjɒnd/	prep.	更远；远于
initially /ɪˈnɪʃəli/	ad.	最初，一开始
fold /fəʊld/	v.	折叠，对折
display /dɪˈspleɪ/	v.	陈列；展示
orderly /ˈɔːdəli/	a.	整齐的；有序的

Phrases & expressions

rely on	依靠，依赖
settle in	迁入，安顿
take breaks	休息
set the tone	奠定基调
free up	解放
be determined to do sth.	下定决心做某事
deal with	处理
call the resources	整合资源
search online for...	在线搜索……
organize... by...	依据……组织……

Reading B

New words

▲urban /ˈɜːbən/	a. 城市的，城镇的	acceleration /əkˌseləˈreɪʃn/	n. 增速，加快；加速性能
*announce /əˈnaʊns/	v. （尤指公开地）宣布，宣告，通告	mobility /məʊˈbɪləti/	n. 活动性；流动性
*create /kriˈeɪt/	v. 创造；创建；创作；发明	*rural /ˈrʊərəl/	a. 乡村的，农村的；似乡村的
▲delivery /dɪˈlɪvəri/	n. 运送，递送，投递	▲migrate /maɪˈɡreɪt/	v. （指人）大批外出；（暂时）移居，迁移
*cushion /ˈkʊʃn/	v. 对（某事物的影响或力量）起缓冲作用	▲urbanization /ˌɜːbənaɪˈzeɪʃn/	n. 城市化；城市化过程
*reflect /rɪˈflekt/	v. 反射（光、热、声等）；反映，映出（影像）	*flow /fləʊ/	v. 流动
		*opportunity /ˌɒpəˈtjuːnəti/	n. 机遇，时机，机会；可能性
*strengthen /ˈstreŋθn/	v. 增强，加强；巩固		
*limited /ˈlɪmɪtɪd/	a. 有限的；不多的，少量的	▲pursuit /pəˈsjuːt/	n. 追求；从事；实行
allocate /ˈæləkeɪt/	v. 分配；分派；拨给，划拨	autonomy /ɔːˈtɒnəmi/	n. 自治，自治权；自主
		*launch /lɔːntʃ/	v. 启动，推出，发起
*resident /ˈrezɪdənt/	n. 居民，住户	*engage /ɪnˈɡeɪdʒ/	v. 雇用；聘用
▲dominant /ˈdɒmɪnənt/	a. 主要的；主导的；占优势的	globally /ˈɡləʊbəli/	ad. 全球地；全局地；世界上
*promote /prəˈməʊt/	v. 促进；促销，推销；推广	*risk /rɪsk/	n. 风险；危险
*percent /pəˈsent/	n. 百分之……（符号为%）	*insurance /ɪnˈʃʊərəns/	n. 保险
		*benefit /ˈbenɪfɪt/	n. 利益，好处；优势
*appropriate /əˈprəʊpriət/	a. 适当的，恰当的；合适的	*regulation /ˌreɡjuˈleɪʃn/	n. 规则，条例，法规；控制，管理
*utilize /ˈjuːtəlaɪz/	v. 使用；利用；应用	*interest /ˈɪntrəst/	n. 利益，好处
		▲vulnerable /ˈvʌlnərəbl/	a. 易受伤的；易受影响的；脆弱的

Phrases & expressions

take up	开始从事；开始学习；拿起	lead to	导致
		launch a business	创业
make it possible (for…) to…	使（某人）做某事成为可能	take the lead	带头，领先

Unit 6

Reading A

New words

*unprecedented /ʌnˈpresɪdentɪd/	a. 前所未有的；没有先例的	lever /ˈliːvə/	n.（车辆或机器的）操纵杆；杠杆
*investment /ɪnˈvestmənt/	n. 投资	multichannel /ˌmʌltɪtʃænl/	a. 多频道的；多通道的
*challenge /ˈtʃælɪndʒ/	n. 挑战	curricula /kəˈrɪkjʊlə/	n. 课程（curriculum 的复数）
*economy /ɪˈkɒnəmi/	n. 经济；经济制度；经济结构	▲augment /ɔːgˈment/	v. 增加；提高；扩大
*consumption /kənˈsʌmpʃn/	n. 消耗；消费	▲collaborative /kəˈlæbərətɪv/	a. 合作的；协作的；协力的
▲innovation /ˌɪnəˈveɪʃn/	n. 创造；创新；改革	▲ecosystem /ˈiːkəʊsɪstəm/	n. 生态系统
▲accelerate /əkˈseləreɪt/	v. 加快；加速	*enhance /ɪnˈhɑːns/	v. 提高；增强；增进
*potentially /pəˈtenʃəli/	ad. 潜在地	▲prospective /prəˈspektɪv/	a. 可能的；预期的；潜在的；即将发生
*manual /ˈmænjuəl/	a. 手工的；体力的	▲incentivize /ɪnˈsentɪvaɪz/	v. 激励；以物质刺激鼓励
*resource /rɪˈsɔːs/	n. 资源；财力	▲incentive /ɪnˈsentɪv/	n. 激励；刺激；鼓励
*ambitious /æmˈbɪʃəs/	a. 有野心的；有雄心的	*prosperity /prɒˈsperəti/	n. 繁荣；成功；昌盛；兴旺
*imply /ɪmˈplaɪ/	v. 含有……的意思；暗示	▲livelihood /ˈlaɪvlihʊd/	n. 赚钱谋生的手段；生计
▲cognitive /ˈkɒgnətɪv/	a. 认知的；感知的	▲hinge /hɪndʒ/	v. 给（某物）装铰链
*identify /aɪˈdentɪfaɪ/	v. 确认；鉴定；找到；发现		

Phrases & expressions

on the rise	增加；提高；好转	as well as	及；既……又……；除……之外（也）
in demand	很受欢迎；需求量大	hinge on	取决于

Reading B

New words

*maximize /ˈmæksɪmaɪz/	v.	充分利用；最大限度地利用	▲asset /ˈæset/	n.	有价值的人（或事物）；资产；财产
*acquire /əˈkwaɪə(r)/	v.	获得	▲expertise /ˌekspɜːˈtiːz/	n.	专门知识；专门技能；专长
unavoidable /ˌʌnəˈvɔɪdəbl/	a.	无法避免的；难以预防的	▲option /ˈɒpʃn/	n.	选择；选择权；选择的自由
▲deliberate /dɪˈlɪbərət/	a.	故意的；蓄意的；存心的；深思熟虑的	unanticipated /ˌʌnænˈtɪsɪpeɪtɪd/	a.	没想到的；未预料到的
▲voluntary /ˈvɒləntri/	a.	自愿的	▲delegate /ˈdelɪgeɪt/	v.	把（工作等）委托（给下级）
▲ancestry /ˈænsestri/	n.	世系；血统			
transferable /trænsˈfɜːrəbl/	a.	可转移的；可转换的			
▲indispensable /ˌɪndɪˈspensəbl/	a.	不可或缺的			

Phrases & expressions

associate sth. with sth.	把两者联系在一起
be motivated to	有动机有积极性做某事
prevent sb. from doing sth.	阻止某人做某事

Glossary

A

			Unit	Reading
absorb /əbˈzɔːb/	v.	吸收（液体、气体等）	1	A
accelerate /əkˈseləreɪt/	v.	加快；加速	6	A
acceleration /əkˌseləˈreɪʃn/	n.	增速，加快；加速性能	5	B
acceptable /əkˈseptəbl/	a.	（社会上）认同的，认可的；可接受的	2	B
acknowledge /əkˈnɒlɪdʒ/	v.	承认；搭理	2	B
acquire /əˈkwaɪə(r)/	v.	获得	6	B
administrative /ədˈmɪnɪstrətɪv/	a.	管理的；行政的	5	A
admiration /ˌædməˈreɪʃn/	n.	钦佩	3	A
aesthetic /iːˈsθetɪk/	n.	（审）美学；美的哲学	1	A
ailment /ˈeɪlmənt/	n.	轻病；小恙	1	A
allocate /ˈæləkeɪt/	v.	分配；分派；拨给，划拨	5	B
ambitious /æmˈbɪʃəs/	a.	有野心的；有雄心的	6	A
amplify /ˈæmplɪfaɪ/	v.	放大，增强	3	B
ancestor /ˈænsestə(r)/	n.	祖宗；祖先	1	B
ancestry /ˈænsestri/	n.	世系；血统	6	B
announce /əˈnaʊns/	v.	（尤指公开地）宣布，宣告，通告	5	B
annual /ˈænjuəl/	a.	每年的；一年一次的；年度的	1	B
appeal /əˈpiːl/	n.	吸引力，魅力	4	A
appear /əˈpɪə(r)/	v.	显得；看来；似乎；出现；呈现；显现	1	B
appetizer /ˈæpɪtaɪzə(r)/	n.	（餐前的）开胃品，开胃饮料	1	B
approach /əˈprəʊtʃ/	v.	靠近；接近	2	B
appropriate /əˈprəʊpriət/	a.	适当的，恰当的；合适的	5	B
aroma /əˈrəʊmə/	n.	芳香；香味	1	A
artifact /ˈɑːtɪfækt/	n.	手工制品，手工艺品	3	A
asset /ˈæset/	n.	有价值的人（或事物）；资产；财产	6	B
associate /əˈsəʊsieɪt/	n.	同事；伙伴；合伙人	2	B

atmosphere /ˈætməsfɪə(r)/	n.	气氛；氛围	4	B
attire /əˈtaɪə(r)/	n.	服装	2	B
attribute /ˈætrɪˌbjuːt/	n.	特征，特性，属性	4	B
augment /ɔːgˈment/	v.	增加；提高；扩大	6	A
auspicious /ɔːˈspɪʃəs/	a.	吉利的；吉祥的	1	B
authentic /ɔːˈθentɪk/	a.	真正的；真实的；逼真的	1	A
authorization /ˌɔːθəraɪˈzeɪʃn/	n.	批准，准许；授权	5	A
autonomy /ɔːˈtɒnəmi/	n.	自治，自治权；自主	5	B
avoid /əˈvɔɪd/	v.	避免；防止；躲避	1	A

B

behave /bɪˈheɪv/	v.	行事，表现	5	A
benefit /ˈbenɪfɪt/	n.	利益，好处；优势	5	B
beyond /bɪˈjɒnd/	prep.	更远；远于	5	A
bonding /ˈbɒndɪŋ/	n.	人与人之间的关系	1	B
	v.	使……结合；使……联结		
broth /brɒθ/	n.	（加入蔬菜的）肉汤，鱼汤	1	B
bubble /ˈbʌbl/	v.	起泡，冒泡	1	B

C

calendar /ˈkælɪndə(r)/	n.	日历；挂历；日程表	1	B
casual /ˈkæʒuəl/	a.	随便的，非正式的	2	B
category /ˈkætəgəri/	n.	（人或事物的）类别，种类	1	A
cautious /ˈkɔːʃəs/	a.	小心的；谨慎的	2	A
celebration /ˌselɪˈbreɪʃn/	n.	庆典；庆祝	3	A
challenge /ˈtʃælɪndʒ/	n.	挑战	6	A
claw /klɔː/	n.	（动物或禽类的）爪；（水生有壳动物的）钳	1	B
cognitive /ˈkɒgnətɪv/	a.	认知的；感知的	6	A
collaborative /kəˈlæbərətɪv/	a.	合作的；协作的；协力的	6	A
commitment /kəˈmɪtmənt/	n.	承诺	2	B
complete /kəmˈpliːt/	v.	完成；完工；使完整	5	A
connotation /ˌkɒnəˈteɪʃn/	n.	内涵	4	B
considerably /kənˈsɪdərəbli/	ad.	非常；很；相当多地	2	B
consistent /kənˈsɪstənt/	a.	一贯的；坚持的；始终如一的	5	A
consumption /kənˈsʌmpʃn/	n.	消耗；消费	6	A
continuity /ˌkɒntɪˈnjuːəti/	n.	连续性；持续性	3	A
correspondence /ˌkɒrəˈspɒndəns/	n.	通信；相似	2	A

counter /ˈkaʊntə(r)/	v.	抵制；抵消	3	B
couplet /ˈkʌplət/	n.	对句（相连的两行长度相等的诗句）；对联	1	B
courteous /ˈkɜːtiəs/	a.	有礼貌的；谦恭有礼的	5	A
craft /krɑːft/	n.	手艺；工艺	3	A
create /kriˈeɪt/	v.	创造；创建；创作；发明	5	B
crisis /ˈkraɪsɪs/	n.	危机	3	B
crucial /ˈkruːʃl/	a.	关键的	2	A
cuisine /kwɪˈziːn/	n.	烹饪；风味	3	A
cure /kjʊə(r)/	v.	治愈，治好（疾病）；解决（问题）	1	A
	n.	药物；疗法；治疗	1	A
curricula /kəˈrɪkjʊlə/	n.	课程（curriculum的复数）	6	A
cushion /ˈkʊʃn/	v.	对（某事物的影响或力量）起缓冲作用	5	B

D

decoration /ˌdekəˈreɪʃn/	n.	装饰品；装饰图案；装饰风格	1	B
delegate /ˈdelɪɡeɪt/	v.	把（工作等）委托（给下级）	6	B
deliberate /dɪˈlɪbərət/	a.	故意的；蓄意的；存心的；深思熟虑的	6	B
deliver /dɪˈlɪvə/	v.	发表	2	B
delivery /dɪˈlɪvəri/	n.	运送，递送，投递	5	B
demographic /ˌdeməˈɡræfɪk/	n.	（尤指特定年龄段的）人群	4	A
demonstrate /ˈdemənstreɪt/	v.	显示；表明	5	A
determination /dɪˌtɜːmɪˈneɪʃn/	n.	决心；毅力	5	A
devastating /ˈdevəsteɪtɪŋ/	a.	毁灭性的	3	A
deviate /ˈdiːvieɪt/	v.	偏离；违背	2	A
devote /dɪˈvəʊt/	v.	将……贡献给，把……奉献给	5	A
diet /ˈdaɪət/	n.	日常饮食；规定饮食（为健康或减肥等目的）		
	v.	节食；按规定饮食	1	A
dip /dɪp/	v.	蘸；浸	1	B
discern /dɪˈsɜːn/	v.	辨别；了解	2	A
display /dɪˈspleɪ/	v.	陈列；展示	5	A
dispute /ˈdɪspjuːt/	n.	纠纷，争端	4	B
diversity /daɪˈvɜːsəti/	n.	多样化	3	A
division /dɪˈvɪʒn/	n.	部门；分开	2	A
dominant /ˈdɒmɪnənt/	a.	主要的；主导的；占优势的	5	B

E

economy /ɪˈkɒnəmi/	n.	经济；经济制度；经济结构	6	A
ecosystem /ˈiːkəʊsɪstəm/	n.	生态系统	6	A
embark /ɪmˈbɑːk/	v.	登上	4	B
emergency /ɪˈmɜːdʒənsi/	n.	突发事件；紧急情况	3	B
engage /ɪnˈgeɪdʒ/	v.	雇用；聘用	5	B
enhance /ɪnˈhɑːns/	v.	提高；增强；增进	6	A
enlightenment /ɪnˈlaɪtənmənt/	n.	启蒙	4	B
ensure /ɪnˈʃʊə(r)/	v.	确保；保证	5	A
entire /ɪnˈtaɪə(r)/	a.	全部的；整个的；完全的	1	B
envelope /ˈenvələʊp/	n.	信封；塑料封套；塑料封皮	1	B
equivalent /ɪˈkwɪvələnt/	a.	（价值、数量、意义、重要性等）相等的，相同的	1	B
error /ˈerə(r)/	n.	错误；差错；谬误	2	A
essential /ɪˈsenʃl/	a.	必要的；必不可少的；根本的	1	A
	n.	必不可少的东西；必需品；要点	1	A
established /ɪˈstæblɪʃt/	a.	已确立的	2	B
ethic /ˈeθɪk/	n.	道德；伦理；行为准则	5	A
etiquette /ˈetɪkət/	n.	礼仪；（社会或行业中的）礼节；规矩	2	A
expertise /ˌekspɜːˈtiːz/	n.	专门知识；专门技能；专长	6	B

F

factor /ˈfæktə(r)/	n.	因素；要素	5	A
far-reaching /ˌfɑːˈriːtʃɪŋ/	a.	深远的	3	B
firecracker /ˈfaɪəkrækə(r)/	n.	鞭炮；爆竹	1	B
fix /fɪks/	n.	（尤指由自己引起的）困境，窘境	2	B
flexibility /ˌfleksəˈbɪləti/	n.	柔韧性；灵活性；弹性	1	B
flow /fləʊ/	v.	流动	5	B
fold /fəʊld/	v.	折叠，对折	5	A
foster /ˈfɒstə(r)/	v.	促进；鼓励	5	A
foul /faʊl/	a.	很令人不快的；下流的	2	B
frustrate /frʌˈstreɪt/	v.	使沮丧	2	A
frustration /frʌˈstreɪʃn/	n.	挫折；沮丧	5	A
fusion /ˈfjuːʒn/	n.	融合；熔接；结合	1	A

G

generation /ˌdʒenəˈreɪʃn/		n.	世，代，辈	4	A
genre /ˈʒɑːnrə/		n.	（文学、艺术、电影或音乐的）体裁，类型	3	A
globally /ˈɡləʊbəli/		ad.	全球地；全局地；世界上	5	B
grant /ɡrɑːnt/		v.	准予，允许	3	A
guarantee /ˌɡærənˈtiː/		v.	保证；担保	3	A
guerilla /ɡəˈrɪlə/		n.	游击队	4	A

H

harmonious /hɑːˈməʊniəs/		a.	友好和睦的；和谐的；协调的	1	B
herb /hɜːb/		n.	药草；香草；草本植物	1	A
hierarchy /ˈhaɪərɑːki/		n.	等级制度（尤指社会或组织）	2	B
hinge /hɪndʒ/		v.	给（某物）装铰链	6	A

I

identify /aɪˈdentɪfaɪ/		v.	确认；鉴定；找到；发现	6	A
ideological /ˌaɪdɪəˈlɒdʒɪkl/		a.	思想观念上的；思想体系的；意识形态的	4	B
impact /ˈɪmpækt/		n.	巨大影响	3	B
imply /ɪmˈplaɪ/		v.	含有……的意思；暗示	6	A
impression /ɪmˈpreʃn/		n.	印象；效果	2	A
incentive /ɪnˈsentɪv/		n.	激励；刺激；鼓励	6	A
incentivize /ɪnˈsentɪvaɪz/		v.	激励；以物质刺激鼓励	6	A
indispensable /ˌɪndɪˈspensəbl/		a.	不可或缺的	6	B
individual /ˌɪndɪˈvɪdʒuəl/		n.	个人	2	A
inferior /ɪnˈfɪəriə/		a.	差的，低等的	4	B
influence /ˈɪnfluəns/		n.	影响；作用；有影响的人（或事物）	1	A
		v.	影响；对……起作用；支配；左右		
ingredient /ɪnˈɡriːdiənt/		n.	成分；（尤指烹饪）原料	1	A
initially /ɪˈnɪʃəli/		ad.	最初，一开始	5	A
innovation /ˌɪnəˈveɪʃn/		n.	创造；创新；改革	6	A
insight /ˈɪnsaɪt/		n.	洞察力	3	B
insurance /ɪnˈʃʊərəns/		n.	保险	5	B
intangible /ɪnˈtændʒəbl/		a.	无形的	3	B
integral /ˈɪntɪɡrəl/		a.	必需的；不可或缺的	1	A
		n.	整体		

integration /ˌɪntɪˈɡreɪʃən/	n.	结合；集成；一体化；整合	4	B	
interconnectedness /ˌɪntəkəˈnektɪdnəs/	n.	关联性	3	B	
interest /ˈɪntrəst/	n.	利益，好处	5	B	
internal /ɪnˈtɜːnl/	a.	内部的，内在的	5	A	
internship /ˈɪntɜːnʃɪp/	n.	（学生或毕业生的）实习期	2	A	
interpretation /ɪnˌtɜːprəˈteɪʃn/	n.	理解；解释	3	A	
inventory /ˈɪnvəntri/	n.	库存	3	A	
investment /ɪnˈvestmənt/	n.	投资	6	A	
issue /ˈɪʃuː/	n.	问题；议题	5	A	

L

launch /lɔːntʃ/	v.	启动，推出，发起	5	B
lever /ˈliːvə/	n.	（车辆或机器的）操纵杆；杠杆	6	A
limited /ˈlɪmɪtɪd/	a.	有限的；不多的，少量的	5	B
limp /lɪmp/	a.	无力的；柔软的	2	B
livelihood /ˈlaɪvlihʊd/	n.	赚钱谋生的手段；生计	6	A
longevity /lɒnˈdʒevəti/	n.	长寿；长命；持久	1	B
loyalty /ˈlɔɪəlti/	n.	忠诚；忠实；忠心耿耿	1	B

M

maintain /meɪnˈteɪn/	v.	维持；保持	3	A
manager /ˈmænɪdʒə(r)/	n.	经理；主管	5	A
Mandarin /ˈmændərɪn/	n.	（中文）普通话	1	B
manner /ˈmænə(r)/	n.	方式，方法	5	A
manual /ˈmænjuəl/	a.	手工的；体力的	6	A
maximize /ˈmæksɪmaɪz/	v.	充分利用；最大限度地利用	6	B
mechanically /mɪˈkænɪkli/	ad.	使用机械地；机动地；在机械方面；机械上；机械地	4	B
mechanism /ˈmekənɪzəm/	n.	方法；机制	3	B
migrate /maɪˈɡreɪt/	v.	（指人）大批外出；（暂时）移居，迁移	5	B
mobility /məʊˈbɪləti/	n.	活动性；流动性	5	B
mobilize /ˈməʊbəlaɪz/	v.	调动；调用	3	B
momentum /məˈmentəm/	n.	动力；势头	3	A
motivation /ˌməʊtɪˈveɪʃn/	n.	积极性，干劲；动机，诱因	5	A
multichannel /ˈmʌltɪtʃænl/	a.	多频道的；多通道的	6	A
myth /mɪθ/	n.	神话	1	B

N

navigate /ˈnævɪgeɪt/	v.	导航；找到正确方法	2	A
negatively /ˈnegətɪvli/	ad.	消极的；负面的	2	A
nomination /ˌnɒmɪˈneɪʃn/	n.	提名；推荐	3	A
nostalgia /nɒˈstældʒə/	n.	怀旧；恋旧	4	A
nuance /ˈnuːɑːns/	n.	细微的差别	2	B
nutritional /njuˈtrɪʃənl/	a.	（食物中）营养的,营养成分的	1	A

O

observe /əbˈzɜːv/	v.	注意到；观察到	2	B
occasion /əˈkeɪʒn/	n.	场合；特别的事情（或仪式、庆典）	1	B
opportunity /ˌɒpəˈtjuːnəti/	n.	机遇,时机,机会；可能性	5	B
option /ˈɒpʃn/	n.	选择；选择权；选择的自由	6	B
oral /ˈɔːrəl/	a.	口头的	3	A
orderly /ˈɔːdəli/	a.	整齐的；有序的	5	A
organizational /ˌɔːgənaɪˈzeɪʃənl/	a.	组织的；机构的	2	B
oversight /ˈəʊvəsaɪt/	n.	监督；监察；监管	5	A

P

pandemic /pænˈdemɪk/	n.	流行病	3	B
participate /pɑːˈtɪsɪpeɪt/	v.	参加；参与	1	B
passionate /ˈpæʃənət/	a.	热情的,狂热的	4	A
patriotism /ˈpeɪtriətɪzəm/	n.	爱国主义	4	B
perceive /pəˈsiːv/	v.	感知；将……理解为	2	A
percent /pəˈsent/	n.	百分之……（符号为%）	5	B
permanent /ˈpɜːmənənt/	a.	永久的；永恒的	2	A
permeate /ˈpɜːmieɪt/	v.	渗透；弥漫；遍布；充满	5	A
policy /ˈpɒləsi/	n.	政策；方针	2	A
positive /ˈpɒzətɪv/	a.	积极乐观的	2	A
possess /pəˈzes/	v.	拥有,具有	5	A
potentially /pəˈtenʃəli/	ad.	潜在地	6	A
powerhouse /ˈpaʊəhaʊs/	n.	强国	4	A
practicability /ˌpræktɪkəˈbɪlɪti/	n.	实用性,可行性	4	B
premise /ˈpremɪs/	n.	（企业或机构使用的）房屋及土地；经营场所	2	B
preparedness /prɪˈpeərɪdnəs/	n.	（尤指对战争或灾难）有准备,做好准备	3	B
presence /ˈprezns/	n.	存在；出现	2	A

preserve /prɪˈzɜːv/	v.	保存，保留	3	A
prevalent /ˈprevələnt/	a.	流行的；普遍存在的；盛行的	1	A
prevent /prɪˈvent/	v.	阻止；阻碍；阻挠	1	A
process /ˈprəʊses/	n.	过程；进程	3	A
productivity /ˌprɒdʌkˈtɪvəti/	n.	生产力；生产率；生产能力	5	A
professionalism /prəˈfeʃənəlɪzəm/	n.	专业水平；专业素质	2	A
profundity /prəˈfʌndɪti/	n.	深度	4	B
prolong /prəˈlɒŋ/	v.	延长	1	B
prominent /ˈprɒmɪnənt/	a.	突出的，显著的	4	B
promote /prəˈməʊt/	v.	促进；促销，推销；推广	5	B
property /ˈprɒpəti/	n.	所有物；财产；不动产	1	A
proposal /prəˈpəʊzl/	n.	建议；计划；提案	5	A
prospective /prəˈspektɪv/	a.	可能的；预期的；潜在的；即将发生	6	A
prosperity /prɒˈsperəti/	n.	繁荣；成功；昌盛；兴旺	6	A
prosperous /ˈprɒspərəs/	a.	繁荣的；成功的；兴旺的	1	B
protein /ˈprəʊtiːn/	n.	蛋白质	1	B
psychological /ˌsaɪkəˈlɒdʒɪkl/	a.	心理的	3	B
punctuality /ˌpʌŋktjuˈælɪti/	n.	准时	2	B
pursuit /pəˈsjuːt/	n.	追求；从事；实行	5	B

R

racial /ˈreɪʃl/	a.	种族的；种族间的；人种的	2	B
radiate /ˈreɪdiˌeɪt/	v.	辐射；发散；从中心发散；呈辐射状发出	4	B
random /ˈrændəm/	a.	任意的；随机的；胡乱的	5	A
rebranding /ˌriːˈbrændɪŋ/	n.	重塑形象	4	A
recreate /ˌriːkriˈeɪt/	v.	再现；再创造	3	A
reflect /rɪˈflekt/	v.	反射（光、热、声等）；反映，映出（影像）	5	B
reflection /rɪˈflekʃn/	n.	反射；显示；表达	2	A
region /ˈriːdʒən/	n.	地区，区域，地方；行政	1	B
regulation /ˌregjuˈleɪʃn/	n.	规则，条例，法规；控制，管理	5	B
rejuvenation /rɪˌdʒuːvəˈneɪʃn/	n.	复兴	4	B
reliance /rɪˈlaɪəns/	n.	依赖	3	B
remedy /ˈremədi/	n.	补救办法；疗法	5	A
represent /ˌreprɪˈzent/	v.	代表；作为……的代言人	1	B
representation /ˌreprɪzenˈteɪʃn/	n.	表现	3	A
require /rɪˈkwaɪə(r)/	v.	需要；要求	5	A
requirement /rɪˈkwaɪəmənt/	n.	要求；必要条件	2	B

resident /ˈrezɪdənt/	n.	居民，住户	5	B
resilience /rɪˈzɪliəns/	n.	恢复力；弹力；适应力	3	B
resource /rɪˈsɔːs/	n.	资源；财力	6	A
restriction /rɪˈstrɪkʃn/	n.	限制	3	B
resurgence /rɪˈsɜːdʒəns/	n.	复苏	4	A
reunion /ˌriːˈjuːniən/	n.	重逢；团聚；聚会；相聚；团圆	1	B
risk /rɪsk/	n.	风险；危险	5	B
ritual /ˈrɪtʃuəl/	a.	庆典的	3	A
rural /ˈruərəl/	a.	乡村的，农村的；似乡村的	5	B

S

safeguard /ˈseɪfɡɑːd/	v.	保护；保障；捍卫	3	B
schedule /ˈʃeduːl/	v.	安排；为……安排时间	2	A
seasoning /ˈsiːzənɪŋ/	n.	调味品；作料	1	B
sexist /ˈseksɪst/	n.	性别歧视者	2	B
shift /ʃɪft/	n.	班；轮班	5	A
shiitake /ʃɪˈtɑːki/	n.	香菇；香蕈	1	B
significant /sɪɡˈnɪfɪkənt/	a.	有重大意义的；显著的	1	B
Sinophone /ˈsaɪnəʊfəʊn/	n.	华语语系；译意风	1	B
snack /snæk/	n.	点心；小吃；快餐	1	B
solely /ˈsəʊlli/	ad.	唯一地	2	B
sophisticated /səˈfɪstɪkeɪtɪd/	a.	复杂的；水平高的	3	A
spark /spɑːk/	v.	引发；触发	3	B
stability /stəˈbɪləti/	n.	稳定性	3	A
staple /ˈsteɪpl/	a.	主要的；基本的；重要的	1	A
strengthen /ˈstreŋθn/	v.	增强，加强；巩固	5	B
subordinate /səˈbɔːdɪnət/	n.	下级；部属	2	A
suits /suːts/	n.	西服；套装	2	B
summarize /ˈsʌməraɪz/	v.	总结；概括；概述	3	B
surge /sɜːdʒ/	n.	激增	4	A
surplus /ˈsɜːpləs/	n.	过剩；剩余；盈余	1	B
	a.	过剩的；剩余的；多余的		
surroundings /səˈraʊndɪŋz/	n.	周围的环境	3	A
sustainable /səˈsteɪnəbl/	a.	可持续的	3	A
sustenance /ˈsʌstənəns/	n.	食物；营养；养料	1	B
symbolic /sɪmˈbɒlɪk/	a.	作为象征的；象征性的	1	B

T

territory /ˈterətri/		n.	领土；版图	3	A
testimony /ˈtestɪməni/		n.	证据；证明	3	B
therapy /ˈθerəpi/		n.	治疗；疗法	1	A
thrive /θraɪv/		v.	兴旺发达；繁荣	3	B
tipsy /ˈtɪpsi/		a.	略有醉意的	2	B
toast /təʊst/		n.	敬酒；祝酒	2	B
toxic /ˈtɒksɪk/		a.	有毒的；引起中毒的	1	A
		n.	毒物；毒剂	1	A
trait /treɪt/		n.	特征，特性，品质	5	A
transferable /trænsˈfɜːrəbl/		a.	可转移的；可转换的	6	B
transmit /trænzˈmɪt/		v.	传输	3	B
treat /triːt/		v.	处理；治疗；把……看作	1	A
tuxedo /tʌkˈsiːdəʊ/		n.	燕尾服	2	B

U

unanticipated /ˌʌnænˈtɪsɪpeɪtɪd/		a.	没想到的；未预料到的	6	B
unavoidable /ˌʌnəˈvɔɪdəbl/		a.	无法避免的；难以预防的	6	B
unexpected /ˌʌnɪkˈspektɪd/		a.	出乎意料的；始料不及的	3	B
unique /juˈniːk/		a.	唯一的；独特的	3	A
unprecedented /ʌnˈpresɪdentɪd/		a.	前所未有的；没有先例的	6	A
urban /ˈɜːbən/		a.	城市的，城镇的	5	B
urbanization /ˌɜːbənaɪˈzeɪʃn/		n.	城市化；城市化过程	5	B
utensil /juːˈtensl/		n.	（家庭）用具，器皿	1	A
utilize /ˈjuːtəlaɪz/		v.	使用；利用；应用	5	B

V

vehicle /ˈviːəkl/		n.	手段，工具	3	A
visibility /ˌvɪzəˈbɪləti/		n.	可见度	3	B
vital /ˈvaɪtl/		a.	必不可少的；对……极重要的；充满生机的	1	A
vitality /vaɪˈtæləti/		n.	活力；生机；生命力；生存力	4	B
voluntary /ˈvɒləntri/		a.	自愿的	6	B
vulnerable /ˈvʌlnərəbl/		a.	易受伤的；易受影响的；脆弱的	5	B

W

wok /wɒk/		n.	炒菜锅	1	A
wrap /ræp/		n.	包裹（或包装）材料	1	B
		v.	包；裹；用……包裹（或包扎、覆盖等）		
wrinkle /ˈrɪŋkl/		n.	（尤指脸上的）皱纹	2	B

Phrases & expressions

A

		Unit	Reading
according to	根据	2	B
adapt... to ...	使……适应……	3	B
appeal to	对……有吸引力	4	A
as long as	只要	4	B
associate sth. with sth.	把两者联系在一起	6	B
as well as	以及；既……又……；除……之（也）	6	A
attach importance to	重视	3	A
a variety of	各种各样的	3	A

B

		Unit	Reading
based on	在……基础上	3	A
be achieving with	用……达到	4	A
be associated with	与……相关；与……联系	1	B
be aware of	意识到，知道	2	A
be confident about	对……有信心	4	A
be determined to do sth.	下定决心做某事	5	A
be divided by	按……划分	1	A
be eager to	渴望	4	B
be inferior to	不如	4	B
be infused with	融入	1	A
be mindful of	注意，留心	2	A
be motivated to	有动机有积极性做某事	6	B
be popular among	受……欢迎	4	A
be regarded as	被认为是；被当作是；视为	1	B
be respectful of	尊重他人	2	A

C

call the resources	整合资源	5	A
common humanity	人道主义，共同人性	3	B
concentrate on	专注于	2	B
consist of	由……组成	1	A
contribute to	贡献	3	B
couple with	与……连接在一起；相伴随	2	B

D

deal with	处理	5	A
define as	界定；定义为	3	A
dress code	着装要求	2	A
due to	由于	4	A

F

free up	解放	5	A

H

highlight the importance of	强调……的重要性	3	B
hinge on	取决于	6	A

I

in addition to	加之；另外；又	1	A
in case	万一；假使	2	B
in demand	很受欢迎；需求量大	6	A
in regard to	至于，关于	2	A
in response to	作为回应	3	A
integrate… into…	与……成为一体	3	B
interact with	互动	2	A
interaction with	与……相互作用	3	A
in the midst of	在……当中	3	B

K

known as	被称为	4	A

L

lead to	导致	5	B
launch a business	创业	5	B

M

make it possible (for…) to…	使（某人）做某事成为可能	5	B
make sure	确保，确信	2	A
make way for	为……开路	1	B

O

on the rise	增加；提高；好转	6	A
organize… by…	依据……组织……	5	A
out of nowhere	突然出现	4	A
outside of fashion	与时尚无关	4	A

P

pass down	传递，传承	2	B
present oneself	展现自我	2	A
prevent sb. from doing sth.	阻止某人做某事	6	B
put in place	就位，启用	3	B

R

recognize as	承认	3	A
recover from	从……恢复	3	B
refer to	查阅，提及	2	B
rely on	依靠，依赖	5	A
result in	导致	3	A

S

seal a deal	达成交易	2	B
search online for…	在线搜索……	5	A
set the tone	奠定基调	5	A
settle in	迁入，安顿	5	A
so as to	以便	3	B
struggle with	与……作斗争	3	B

submit to	呈交	3	A
sweep away	扫清；肃清；冲走	1	B

T

take advantage of	利用	3	B
take breaks	休息	5	A
take effect	生效	3	A
take the lead	带头，为首	5	B
take up	开始从事；开始学习；拿起	5	B
thanks to	幸亏；归因于	3	B

U

under the influence of	在……的影响下	4	B
under your belt	已有的经验和阅历（俚语）	2	A